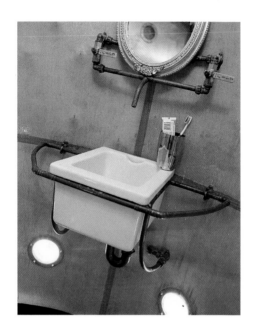

bathrooms

bathrooms

Vinny Lee

photography **Chris Everard**

RYLAND
PETERS
& SMALL

London New York

Designer **Sally Powell**

Senior editor **Henrietta Heald**

Managing editor **Sian Parkhouse**

Location research manager **Kate Brunt**

Location researcher **Sarah Hepworth**

Production manager **Meryl Silbert**

Art director **Gabriella Le Grazie**

Publishing director **Alison Starling**

Stylist **Lucy Gibbons**

First published in the USA in 2000
This revised edition published in 2006 by
Ryland Peters & Small, Inc.
519 Broadway
5th Floor
New York, NY 10012

Text © Vinny Lee 2000, 2006
Design and photographs
© Ryland Peters & Small 2000, 2006
10 9 8 7 6 5 4 3 2 1

Printed and bound in China.

To AWJ, my companion in life's bubbly tub

ISBN-10: 1-84597-246-5
ISBN-13: 978-1-84597-246-2

A CIP record for this book is available from
The Library of Congress.

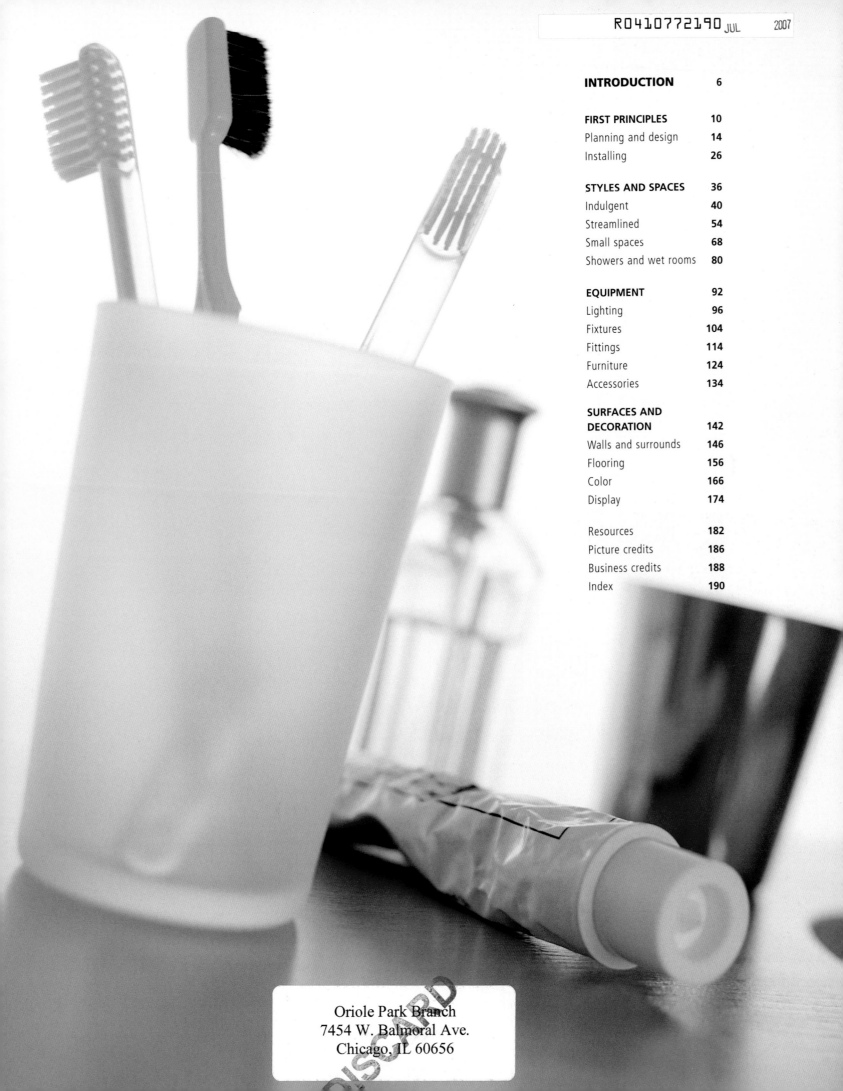

introduction

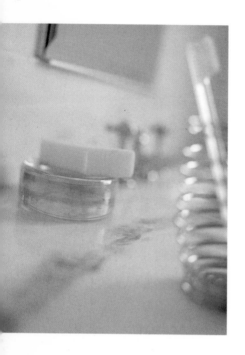

There is more to bathing than simply getting clean. In addition to giving you time to yourself, it can be therapeutic, reviving for jaded spirits, calming, and relaxing. The room in which these activities takes place is one of the most intimate spaces in the home, where decoration and design can enhance the pleasures enjoyed within.

The act of bathing, rather than just washing, was popular among the ancient Egyptians, Greeks, and Romans. The Romans built large communal baths, which included massage areas and steam rooms. However, for much of history, the pleasures of the bath were largely shunned in the West because they were associated with licentiousness and sensuality rather than cleanliness and health. Times have changed. These days, especially in summer, some people shower two or three times a day to refresh and cool themselves.

Direct water supply and drainage became more widely available in prosperous Western countries at the end of the 19th century. Individual municipalities across the USA took responsibility for piping clean running water to most houses, and efficient sewage systems took waste away. The health benefits of washing were also acknowledged. Although many richer households and grand hotels had bathrooms, it was not until after World War I that such facilities were commonplace. Toilets were plumbed inside the house instead of out in the yard, and most new homes were built with designated bathroom spaces. Until then most bathing had taken place in a portable metal bathtub, or consisted of a scrub with a pitcher of water and a bowl to stand in, often in front of the kitchen range.

Early bathrooms were functional places, with linoleum on the floor and tiles or other waterproof protection around the bathtub. Baths were taken once a week, and hair washing became a ritual Friday night activity. Hot water—regarded as a luxury in the financially restrained times of the late 1940s and 1950s—was used sparingly. Today the

bathroom is as much part of the home as any other room, and worries about water usage are more environmental than economic. Decoration is carefully planned, and furniture and fixtures are thoughtfully chosen. From the 1960s, the advent of new materials and a more adventurous aesthetic sense saw bathroom styles and colors change considerably.

Among the many new ideas to be gleaned from cultures where bathing has always been a part of daily life is the belief that bathing should never be rushed. It should be a long, luxurious ritual that may involve two, three, or more processes. Where possible, it should also be a communal and sociable affair. In the Scandinavian sauna, for example, the participants sit or lie on wooden benches. Traditionally, when they have perspired enough, they roll in the snow outside or hose themselves down with cold water to close the pores of the skin that have been opened by the warmth. The heat of the sauna is enhanced by a small open brazier of hot coals onto which water is poured. Essences such as eucalyptus or pine can also be added to mingle with the steam. Some people scrub themselves with birch twigs, which are abrasive and also have a mild scent.

The practice of varying temperatures while bathing, found in both the sauna and the Turkish bath, can be traced back to Roman times, when the public baths were divided into three sections: the tepidarium, the caldarium, and the frigidarium—temperatures varied between warm and icy cold, so the ambience changed from balmy and relaxing to bracing and stimulating, benefitting both the skin and the circulation. This experience can easily be replicated in the modern bathroom. Sitting in a well-sealed shower with hot water pumping out of the shower head, you will be exposed to raised levels of both temperature and steam; with a turn of the dial, the water can be changed to cold, which will do much to invigorate the systems of the body.

1
first principles

planning and design

installing

THE FIRST PROPER BATHROOMS EMERGED IN LATE VICTORIAN TIMES—SMALL,

FUNCTIONAL, ROOMS NOT MUCH WIDER THAN THE WIDTH OF THE TUB WITH THE

TOILET ON ONE SIDE, AND RARELY LONGER THAN THE LENGTH OF THE BATHTUB WITH

SPACE FOR A SINK TO BE PLUMBED IN AT ITS END. DECORATION WAS SIMPLE AND

MUNDANE—WITH WHITE OR OFF-WHITE STANDARD-SHAPED BATHTUBS AND CLASSIC

CERAMIC SINKS. THE BATHROOM OF THIS ERA WAS ENTIRELY UTILITARIAN, AND

THERE WAS LITTLE SPACE FOR MORE THAN ONE PERSON TO WASH AT A TIME.

Today's bathroom is an increasingly important room—and planning and creating a bathroom that fulfills

all your needs is a demanding task. While still primarily a place in which to bathe or shower, a bathroom

may double as an exercise area, a dressing room, or even a laundry—requiring space to accommodate

a rowing machine or an aerobic step, cabinets and chests of drawers, or a washing machine and a

dryer with their associated ducts and pipes. Medicines and cosmetics are often stored and applied or

administered in a bathroom; beauty treatments are carried out there; and for those indulging in a relaxing

soak it may also be a place simply to listen to music, read a book, or sip a glass of wine.

More and more people are installing extra bathrooms in their homes. For example, a family with

children who must be ready for school at the same time as their parents leave for work may find multiple

bathrooms a necessity rather than a luxury. Modern technological developments mean that showers and

separate toilets can be plumbed into closets or into the often-useless sloping area under a staircase.

Bathrooms with a connecting door to the bedroom are also popular, and some people sacrifice a spare

bedroom in favor of a spacious extra bathroom. Whether you are remodeling an existing bathroom,

making a new one, or contemplating adding a secondary washing facility, good preparation is essential.

Care in the early stages will save you time, money, and headaches later. Even if you are working with an architect, interior designer or bath designer, it is useful to have established in your own mind what you hope to achieve in the finished room, and an awareness of the wide number of options in equipment, surfaces, and decoration will give you the confidence to make balanced and informed decisions.

One way of increasing your knowledge and keeping up to date with technological advances is to read some recent issues of specialized bathroom magazines. Bath showrooms are also a useful point of reference—they often have display models that you can see in action. New bathtub shapes and sizes, shower heads and water heaters, finishes, materials, and lighting regularly come onto the market. If you make a habit of assembling manufacturers' pamphlets giving sizes and measurements, you will build up an invaluable file of technical information. There is also a lot of practical advice about bathrooms available on the internet.

Safety concerns should be addressed at each stage of design, planning, and installation of a bathroom, for it is a place where you are potentially very vulnerable, where your skin is unprotected, and the dangers from sharp objects, hot pipes, slippery mats, and hard surfaces are ever-present.

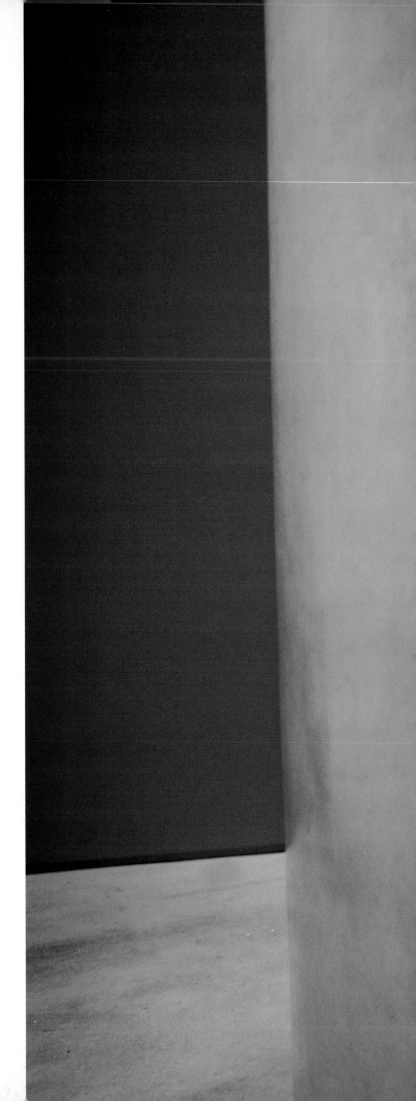

planning and design

Whether you are planning to create a completely
new bathroom, remodeling an old one, or installing
additional fixtures, start by figuring out how much
space you have to play with, and then make a list
of your objectives and priorities.

If you are handy with a pencil and graph paper, you might try drawing
a floor plan. If not, don't worry—many large bathroom suppliers offer a
computer design service that will enable you to see how various styles
of bathroom fixtures can be arranged within the confines of your room.
But you will need to sketch a rough outline of the room, with door and
window positions indicated, and to take measurements of the distances
between the door and the corner of the room, the window height, and
so on, so the computer can be programmed with accurate figures.

When you are calculating the cost of the building work and fixtures,
remember to reserve some of your budget for decoration. A bathroom
can be one of the most satisfying rooms to decorate. Its relative smallness
means that it can be finished more quickly than a larger room, and you
can introduce ideas and materials that might be regarded as too expensive
or flamboyant for a more public space.

Identifying your needs

The next stage is to decide exactly what you need. Is the aim to create
a main bathroom or an additional facility to satisfy competing demands?
Can the various washing needs be divided between two spaces or more?
How many people will be using the facilities?

Young children, elderly people, and people with disabilities have special
requirements. For example, anyone who uses a wheelchair needs more
space to maneuver, and grab rails to help with getting in and out or up
and down. Wall-hung sinks and toilets are useful for disabled people
because the lack of a pedestal gives easier and closer access to the bowl.
Nonslip flooring is of crucial importance for those whose youth or frailty
means that they are unsteady on their feet. Bathing can be especially

**Simple shapes can look dramatic in plain, uncluttered
surroundings. This graceful curved sink and simple wall-
mounted spout are practical but also attractive. When
planning and installing your bathroom, start with less
and build up to more, rather than the other way around.**

Left **Provide plenty of easily accessible storage and aim to keep surfaces free of clutter. This strategy will not only make it easier to wipe the surfaces clean, but will also add to the aesthetic appearance of the room, especially if it is a modern, streamlined design.**

Above and right **Large tiles can be used to create an illusion of space. They are now available in a variety of materials that were once confined to outdoor settings —for example, slate, limestone, and sandstone, which have inherent waterproof properties and can be finished with a smooth or polished surface.**

challenging for elderly people or those with conditions such as arthritis —although the warmth and relaxing effect of a bath can bring great benefits, the effort of bathing may be a strain. One inexpensive solution is a bath board—a simple but specially designed benchlike seat that lies across the top rim of the tub; this device is not altogether satisfactory, however, because the body of the bather is not immersed.

Also on the market are retractable bands that act as a hoist seat—they can be automatically and mechanically raised and lowered as needed. Hydraulic chairs with hand-operated controls are among the easiest to use but can be expensive to buy and install. Walk-in bathtubs that offer a combination of bath and shower are also widely available. The walk-in bath is a hybrid of a shower cubicle and a small bathtub with a built-in seat. You enter by a low door at the front, which closes tightly to create a deep but upright bathing space.

Bathrooms designed for those with impaired physical ability do not need to be clinical or ugly. Wall grips can be disguised as soap dishes and low-height bathtubs can look elegant rather than specially plumbed in for a geriatric patient. Thermostatic valves and faucets on the tub can be preset to a maximum temperature that the bather feels comfortable with, so there is no risk of scalding. These controls are also ideal for bathrooms used by children because the water temperature can be set below the level at which they might sustain a scald.

Children and teenagers

Children, especially babies and toddlers, need to be kept warm during and after bathing, so adequate heating is important. The bathtub should have a nonslip base and be easily accessible for people who are supervising washing and bathtime. Bathtubs with built-in seats to one side are ideal for toddlers, who can sit there comfortably and be showered or sponged off, rather than sitting or lying vulnerably on the base of a large tub. Bathtubs for young children should be filled with only a few inches of water so their faces are well above the water level if they slip or slide in the bath. Never leave a baby or toddler alone in the bathroom.

If your home is on two or more levels, it is an advantage to have a separate powder room or half-bath on a level other than where the bathroom is located. Such an arrangement can save time and effort for adults, and in a household with small children having a toilet on the same floor of the house as the main living rooms, kitchen, and/or play area takes away the need to carry babies and supervise tots up and down stairs, and makes toilet training less of a trial.

Teenagers may feel shy about their changing bodies and prefer not to share the bathroom with others. They are also notorious for spending an inordinate length of time in the bathroom—a strange turn of events from their childhood, when bathtime was often the most hated part of the day. To resolve this situation you could install a small extra bathroom for their exclusive use.

Exercise and meditation

Keep-fit and exercise facilities can also be located in the bathroom if there is room for them. After rigorous exercise it is very satisfying to be able to step straight into a cooling and cleansing shower or warm bath. Floor and aerobic exercises can take place on a soft padded mat or with weights, but an exercise machine with electrical parts should be kept well away from any contact with water, and the room should be well ventilated to prevent the machine from getting damp. If you are thinking about putting this type of machine in your bathroom, consult the manufacturer or a licensed electrician.

The simple, clean, and private environment of the bathroom can also be conducive to practicing meditation and yoga. When you are physically cleansed and in a relaxed frame of mind, you may find that allowing time to clear your mind is also beneficial. A lightly padded mat can make lying

on the floor more comfortable, or—if you have enough room to spare —a futon-style day bed or chaise would be a luxurious addition. If you are leaving upholstered furniture, padded mats, or pillows in the room for any length of time, make sure the ventilation is effective enough to extract the damp and steam generated by showering or bathing, so the fabrics do not become damp and moldy.

If your dream is to have private and uninterrupted access to your own bathroom, you may need either to knock through a wall to a next-door room or re-use existing space such as a built-in closet, an archway, or a recess. One attraction of a connecting bathroom is that it is reserved primarily for your and your partner's use and enjoyment.

Assessing the options

When you have a general idea of the facilities you would like to install, start collecting pamphlets and catalogs and visiting relevant showrooms. There are numerous makes and brands of fixture, and developments in technology and mass production mean that there is a wider choice than ever of affordable bathrooms. Once regarded as elitist, spas and other devices that deliver water in the form of therapeutic massage jets are now much easier to find.

After surveying the market and establishing the costs, colors, and installation requirements of various items, you can start more detailed planning. Discuss your plans with a builder, contractor, carpenter, electrician, and/or plumber, depending on the scale of the job, and get their input and ideas, as well as estimated costs. The styles and shapes of fixtures on the market range from the traditional to the ultramodern—

Above **Double sinks can be useful in a bathroom used regularly by two people, especially in the morning rush to get ready for work. The plan shown here brings together hard and soft elements. Cool steel sinks are set in a rich warm cherrywood counter with matching backsplash, which also echoes the color and material used for the floor.**

Left and opposite page, near right **Where space is limited, one solution is to combine some facilities by installing, for example, a combination shower and tub, or a toilet with a bidet-style shower attachment. Hair washing can be made easier by wall-mounting a waterspout above a sink.**

Opposite page, top **As long as your bathroom is not overlooked, curtains or shades may be needed only to give you a feeling of privacy at night, when it is dark outside. Otherwise, if you have a view, make the most of it. Here a mirrored wall is used to enhance the impact of a wonderful vista of the New York City skyline, as well as to provide a waterproof setting for a shower.**

Opposite page, far right **Connecting bathrooms are always popular. Among their advantages is the fact that you can get dressed immediately after washing without having to go to another room.**

from countertop or set-in vanity units to small hand-rinse sinks for half-baths, and from reproductions of traditional toilets with the tank wall-mounted high above the bowl and flushed by a handle on a metal chain to the sleekest bowl with concealed tank. Bathtubs are manufactured in various materials from rigid acrylic to cast iron and pressed steel, and from the classic rolltop to the standard oblong, as well as the sculpted corner version.

Try not to be overwhelmed by the choice, but be rigorous about dismissing those items you are not certain about and keep notes about those with outstanding appeal. Budgetary and space constraints will help to whittle down the choice.

It is advisable to make a careful study of the dimensions and scale of each item. A corner bathtub might appear to save space, but may in fact take up more room than a standard one. In some cases, the actual bathing space within the area may be the same as, if not smaller than, a standard bathtub, but the curved fascia and corner paneling can mean that the bath extends farther into the room—and occupies more space—than a regular oblong tub would.

There is not only a multitude of styles, colors, and finishes to choose from, but also modern innovations such as pressure-balancing water-control valves, and whirlpool tubs complete with television monitors and stereo CD systems. In these more environmentally conscious times there are also a variety of water purification systems available, and numerous energy-saving devices, including pedestal sinks with faucets designed to use less water. The introduction of a mandatory low-volume flush on toilets—up to a maximum of 1.6 gallons—has led to the design of

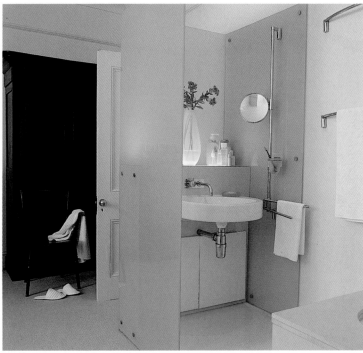

Above **In a large indulgent bathroom, the impact of the fixtures can be softened by setting them against painted walls and textured floor coverings. These classic pedestal sinks with raised curved outlines have a period feel that complements the chest of drawers, the towel ring, and the simple circular mirrors.**
Right **Some fixtures resemble items of furniture, with a flat, tablelike top, and legs rather than a pedestal base.**

pressure-assisted toilets. While generally more efficient than toilets that rely on gravity, pressure-assisted toilets are of variable quality and need to be carefully chosen. Their noisiness and comparatively high price are compensated by cheaper water bills.

You may find the technicalities of this kind of equipment a little bewildering, but take home a pamphlet to read or to discuss with your plumber or builder. Remember that, although gadgets and electronic wizardry may initially seem very appealing, the more items of that sort that you have installed, the more there is that can potentially go wrong, and in a bathroom, where any electrical fixtures and wiring should be safely concealed, it could be difficult to obtain access to them without having to disrupt other objects in the room.

Making the most of a spacious bathroom

The enormous popularity of the indulgent retro look—and, at the other end of the scale, the desire for increasingly powerful and more sophisticated showers, steam baths and whirlpool tubs—means that ever larger spaces are needed to accommodate ornately styled, classical white porcelain fixtures and substantial items of furniture, in addition to the latest hi-tech equipment. If you have a connecting bathroom, it may be possible to enlarge it by taking some extra space from the bedroom to create a truly luxurious master bath suite.

Even in a spacious bathroom, however, detailed planning is important. If two people need to use the bathroom at the same time, a pair of lavs can help speed up the washing routine in the mornings and evenings. Generous storage, including built-in drawers, does much to enhance the room's usefulness. Individual cabinets installed above or below the basins mean that each person's particular toothbrush, toothpaste, deodorant, and other toiletries can be kept readily at hand.

One way of dealing with competing demands on a large bathroom is to subdivide the space and give definition to separate areas—a plan that can be enhanced by careful positioning of lighting. This allows different fixtures to be used at the same time without too much intrusion on privacy—for example, one person could use the shower while another person is using the vanity area.

More permanent subdivisions can also be introduced into a large space. For example, a wall or half-wall can be constructed to enclose the area around the bathtub, making it cozier, and decorated to create an intimate and indulgent room within a room.

Sinks can be screened from the bathtub or shower enclosure by a wall of glass blocks, which will allow light to travel through them and provide a certain amount of obscurity. Glass blocks have a watery appearance and are sturdy without appearing too dense or solid.

If you are not in favor of installing a permanent surround, a simple movable screen or even a decorative shower curtain on a pole can be used to create a more snug environment. Freestanding or floating walls are a popular foil in large rooms. One side of the wall is frequently used to provide a backsplash for a shower, while the bathtub is plumbed in on the other side—so each fixture is obscured from the other. This type of feature can create a particularly dramatic and arresting effect in minimalist bathrooms or wet rooms where the wall surfaces are covered in a single color or finish.

In a spacious bathroom the toilet and bidet may be concealed in a ventilated enclosure, so they appear to be absent from the room. This provides privacy when the facilities are in use, and it also means that there is easy access to the remainder of the bathroom. A hidden cabinet is another discreet form of disguise—the exterior of the cabinet can be decorated in such a way that it becomes virtually invisible within the overall scheme of the walls.

Below **This old-fashioned, high-level toilet with its raised water tank and wooden seat has a strong period character that has been deliberately reflected in the choice of decor. The floor is wood, and the walls have been wood-paneled and painted in a single, plain color. The classic column radiator serves both as a source of heat and as a convenient towel rod.**

Strategies for a small room

If you lack space in a bathroom, there is an abundance of imaginative, sometimes surprising, solutions to the problem, including many fixtures that have been specially designed for small rooms. For example, one way to add interest to a small bath is to erect a partition or low wall.

Frequently the most economical way of using the floor area in a narrow bathroom is to arrange the fixtures according to a linear scheme, in which the tub and integral shower, with its curtain or glass panel, is placed in the corner at the far end from the door, with the toilet beside it and the sink at its end. Although this is a rather conventional layout, it can be made less so—if there is enough space—by building a mid-height, low wall at the open end of the tub. The wall will not only contain the

bathing area but also provide an extended backsplash around a sink. Another low wall could be constructed to separate the side of the tub from the toilet, providing more privacy to both areas.

There are minor but often overlooked ways in which you can add precious inches to a room. For example, you may gain space in the dead area behind the main door to the room by hanging it so it opens out rather than in—but make sure you have enough space outside the door to allow people to pass comfortably, and check that the opened door will not block off the whole area. By choosing a wall-mounted lav rather than one that has been set into a vanity unit, you will be able to make use of the extra inches on each side of the sink. If you are plumbing a

ceramic fixture behind a door, select a rounded-corner sink rather than a square one so the door is less likely to bang against the edge of the fixture and damage it. A standard-sized sink may not always be necessary. For example, in a half-bath used by guests or a spare bedroom, where washing hands and brushing teeth are the main activities, a smaller rinse-basin will probably be adequate. Alternatively, you could plumb the back of the toilet and tank into an area of restricted height, while the sitting or standing area in front of it is sited in a part of the room where the ceiling gradually rises to full height. If you want to install any fixture in a restricted space, check with your builder or contractor that your plans do not violate building or plumbing codes.

To satisfy increasing demand for smaller units and fixtures that can be used in small or secondary bathrooms, manufacturers have developed lines specifically to fit these spaces. For example, there are small but deep bathtubs, triangular shower cubicles built to fit into corners, or totally enclosed tube-shaped pods with integral shower pans. A more detailed discussion of equipment for small spaces appears on pages 68-78.

For any washing facilities in a restricted space, adequate ventilation is very important. Damp and moisture will accumulate quickly but are slow to disperse, and may cause damage in the long term unless they are efficiently expelled or ducted away.

Opposite page **Three views of the same bathroom show how circular windows and carefully placed mirrors, lights, and ornaments can offset the potentially harsh effect created by the boxy, angular shapes of the bath, the sink unit, and the dividing wall separating the shower enclosure from the rest of the room.** This page **In these bathrooms, by contrast, the angular lines of the fixtures have been emphasized with oblong mirrors, long slatted blinds, linear wooden decking beside the bathtub, a partition with square glass panels, and linear towel rods.**

Adding facilities to an existing room

Some people incorporate washing facilities in a part of the home also used for other purposes. For example, the bathroom or a toilet and sink may be part of a utility room where laundry is done. The room will already be decorated to withstand steam, moisture, and temperature variations, and much of the plumbing, pipes, and wiring necessary for the installation of bathroom fixtures will be in place. There are obvious advantages to keeping washing machines and toilets together in one area.

If you intend to install a small half-bath with a toilet and sink near an area where food is customarily prepared or eaten, make sure the ventilation arrangements comply with building codes. Efficient ventilation and heating systems should always form part of the overall building plan, but they are particularly important in a bathroom that, for example, also serves as a dressing room or is used for the regular storage of bedlinens and towels. To prevent these fabrics from becoming damp and eventually succumbing to mildew, it is necessary to promote vigorous circulation of air through the room.

A dressing room is often located near the bathroom for convenience of use, and sometimes this can offer an unexpected advantage, in that materials such as wrinkled silk or velvet benefit from being allowed to hang temporarily in a steamy place—this is because the warmth and moisture help to relax the fabric and encourage the creases to drop out.

Other practical considerations

There are a number of other practical matters that should be addressed in the early stages of planning a bathroom. For example, if you plan to put a cast-iron bathtub in an upper room, check with the builder or architect that the weight of the tub combined with the weight of the bather and the water when it is filled will not be too heavy for the floor to support. If there is any doubt, you may need to reinforce the ceiling joists of the room below to carry the load.

If you are intending to install a wet room—a dedicated shower room with a graduated floor and a single water drain—check that the weight of the tiles is not likely to create a problem, especially if you are using something as substantial as slate.

In preparation for constructing a wet room, it is important to make sure the walls, floor, and ceiling can be adequately waterproofed and that the waste water will be efficiently piped away from the drain. This may be difficult to achieve in an upper-floor room unless you are also prepared to go to the trouble of constructing a false floor under which the piping can be laid.

Although it may initially seem to be a cheap option, relocating existing fixtures can in fact be more expensive and inconvenient than installing new ones, because the old item or items will have to be disconnected before being taken elsewhere. Existing pipes will also need to be closed off before fixtures are moved.

When choosing your fixtures, favour styles that are appropriate to the setting. For example, the more ornate and delicate items such as glass sinks are probably better suited to an adults' connecting bath, where they will not suffer as much harsh treatment as they would in a communal family bathroom.

The selection and positioning of the various items in a bathroom should take account of cleaning as well as wear and tear. You may conclude that one of the modern wall-hung toilets with a concealed water tank is particularly appropriate in a family bath. Wall-hung toilets offer easy access for cleaning around the base; there is no pedestal and no niches where dust can gather, and the hidden tank does not need to be regularly wiped.

When you are planning this type of installation, remember that, if the tank is concealed behind paneling, access will be necessary in case of plumbing problems—so you need to make sure there is a removable section within the paneling. Indeed, all electrical, mechanical and plumbing systems should be covered by protective panels that can be easily removed. General safety considerations in bathrooms are dealt with on page 28 and elsewhere throughout the book.

You may also want to think about whether to vary the levels within a room. For example, creating a step up to the tub can give a feeling of luxury and may also be a useful way of concealing ugly or intrusive pipework—but take care that it does not become a safety hazard.

Above The choice of materials for surface areas needs careful thought. The top priority is that any such material should be waterproof and resilient to temperature changes and steam. Stone is a naturally weather-proof material that can, with underfloor heating, be made to feel comfortable under bare feet.
Right Stone corners or edges like this one should be rounded to prevent injury. This particularly applies to shelves and to bathtubs and sinks.

Unusual building materials can also be effective in a bathroom. For example, this clear corrugated sheeting is more often found on the roofs of garden sheds and industrial warehouses than in indoor situations, but it has all the qualities required to make it a useful and intriguing screen for a tub and as a partition.

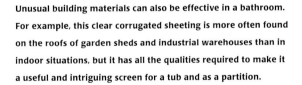

A "sunken" bathtub does not have to be sunk into the floor—you can bring the floor up to meet it, and create the impression that the tub is sunken by building steps up to the surround. The addition of this sort of feature can give a fresh appearance and feel to an existing room without involving you in the trouble and expense of having to replumb or relocate the tub.

installing

Once you have devised a floor plan, the next step is to tackle the technical and practical elements of installing a bathroom. You need not know everything about wiring diagrams and plumbing regulations, but it is useful to be aware of the pros and cons of different systems and the main safety requirements.

Far left The slope-sided stainless steel sink and the mirrors above it were custom-made for this bathroom, but these modern features are teamed with classic elements such as the Pietra Santa limestone flooring and a 1930s magnifying mirror found in a flea market.

Below left and below A simple spout has been set into the countertop at the side of the sink, rather than behind it in the more conventional position. This leaves the surface free in front of the mirror, giving the person using the sink a clearer view.

Bottom left In this small bathroom a faucet has been set on the far side of the sink from the toilet so that it does not intrude upon the area where someone may wish to sit.

Knowing in advance about the sort of problems that might arise can save time and money. You should make allowances in your building schedule for technical hitches and overlapping work—the kind of thing that happens when the wiring needs to be put in before the tiles can be laid, or the plumber needs to install the faucet at the same time as the sink, which is not due to arrive for two weeks. Organizing various workers to come at the right time, and for different items to be delivered when needed, is like fitting the pieces of a jigsaw.

Position is not the only thing to consider when installing the items in a bathroom—height is important, too. For example, tall people may find less strain on the lower back if the sink is placed at their hip to waist height rather than at a standard height. This may mean either building a false base to raise the pedestal or choosing a sink that can be mounted on a wall or set into a vanity unit. The direction in which the cabinet doors open is also worth thinking about. If the doors open out onto each other, it can be difficult to reach the contents of the cabinet; if the doors clash with those of the shower cubicle or the main door of the bathroom, there may be accidents when they are in use at the same time. If you foresee a problem, check with a supplier whether the shower is available with a door that opens in the opposite direction, or ask a contractor whether it would be feasible to hang the cabinet doors from the other side.

Acquaintance with some of the complications of installation and with a few of the more general technical terms means you can ask relevant questions when you are buying fixtures and appliances, and also talk

Above **Wall-mounted faucets and spouts should be carefully installed, and the stone or tiles in which they are set need to be professionally cut.** Right **Stainless steel used to be thought of as an almost exclusively** **industrial material. It was used for washing facilities only in such institutions as army barracks, but it is now increasingly accepted as a practical and chic material for fixtures in the home.**

with some authority to the people who will install them. Do not be afraid to ask questions—and before paying a deposit for any job, make sure you have a clear understanding of what has been agreed.

Safety

Any task involving possible contact between water and electricity should be carried out by a professional who is registered with a recognized organization, and licensed by the state they work in. Use only moisture-proof fixtures specifically designed for bathrooms—light bulbs should be encased in sealed units that protect the fixture from condensation. No lighting fixture, including hanging fixtures, should be within reach of any person who may be standing or seated in the vicinity of the shower or bathtub. Bathroom heaters must also comply with safety codes.

To prevent electrical shocks, all electric outlets should be protected by a Ground Fault Circuit Interrupter (GFCI) device. If an imbalance occurs in the current moving through the electrical circuit, the GFCI stops current flow immediately.

Good illumination in a bathroom is important for safety reasons as well as practical ones. When you are planning the room, make sure all the functional areas will be well provided with natural or artificial light. Where possible, the room should include a window or skylight whose size is equivalent to at least one tenth of the floor area. Handles on doors, cabinets and drawers, and other controls and switches, should be easy to operate with one hand, and should not be placed in any position where they could cause an injury.

In a household that includes young children, bathroom features should include safety latches on cabinets and doors, secure storage for cleaning supplies, and pressure-balancing valves that regulate the water temperature in the shower.

Plumbing

Plumbing is another specialized job that is best done by a professional. Leaking pipes and incorrectly installed joints and overflows can cause spills and drips that may damage walls and floors, leading to rot and even in severe cases to the loss of a floor or ceiling.

Pipes in a bathroom should be carefully positioned, and hot pipes should be insulated, or covered, and if possible boxed in, to keep in the heat. If the hot pipes are in an area where they could accidentally come into contact with bare skin, they should be covered to remove the danger of any burns.

The vogue for freestanding bathtubs and sinks means that such fixtures may be placed in the center of a room, or at some distance from the wall, so water pipes have to be laid across the room from the wall where they are normally fed in. To accommodate this type of plumbing, it is necessary to lift the floor—while it is up, you might want to take the opportunity to put in underfloor heating. If you are installing a

Right and opposite page
From the wide choice of faucets and spouts, try to pick a style that not only complements the design of the fixtures but also fits comfortably with the shape and size of your hands. The configurations of faucets, drains, and plugs also vary. If the spout will not be installed in the conventional place—in the center back of the basin—it is important to make sure the flow of water has direct and easy access to the drain and does not cause splashing.

whirlpool or spa bathtub, choose a system with rigid pipework—which allows the water to drain away completely. Flexible pipework sometimes sags, allowing the dirty water to settle in the pipes and be pumped back into the tub next time it is used. Also, if the tub remains unused for some time, the dirty water may become stagnant and start to smell.

Before installing an old or antique bathtub or sink, check whether it has an overflow outlet—some old tubs and sinks were filled and emptied by hand. If there isn't an overflow in your antique tub, you may want to have one added when the tub is installed.

Tiling and sealing

Water will seep anywhere it can, through cracks and openings of any size, so it is important to seal surfaces that are prone to splashing and those that are in regular contact with moisture. If water seeps behind a bathtub and settles on wooden floorboards, they may become saturated and in time start to rot; the same applies to the splash zone of a sink or even a toilet.

There are many sealants and caulks on the market, some in squeeze-on application tubes, others in the form of a syringe. Most sealants come in a choice of colors designed to match the standard colors of manufactured

fixtures; but if you can't match the color exactly, there is also tub and tile caulk that dries to a transparent finish. You may want to apply caulk to large pieces of equipment such as the bathtub. Caulk has some "give," which is necessary in certain situations—for example,

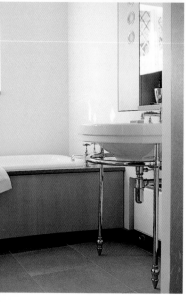

Above **Sinks can be set into a counter similar to a kitchen work surface. Alternatively, they can be also be under-mounted so the upper surface is smooth and easy to clean. In a small room this arrangement may provide useful storage space in cabinets built under and on each side of the sink.**

Left **Traditional basins, such as this one with an integral chrome towel rod, are often set on pedestals or stands.**

when someone gets into a bathtub, the combined weight of human and water may cause the tub to move a little. When the bather gets out and the water has flowed away, the tub may rise a bit and return to its previous position. This movement will weaken any rigid join between the bathtub and the wall.

If the tub is made of cast iron or some other solid material, it may not be affected by such pressure, but the floor on which it is resting, especially if it is a wood one, may sag a little under the weight and then rise again. The movement may be imperceptible, but over time a rigid sealer such as grout would start to crack, and the gap between the bathtub and wall would gradually open up.

Many older homes have walls that are neither perfectly level nor straight. This can cause problems when large areas are tiled because you may find that, if you start in the corner and work across the wall, building row upon row of tiles, your lines become less and less regular. It is a good idea to start in the center of the wall and work out, following a plumb line rather than relying on the baseboard or the corners of the walls to guide

Below and right **Faucets and spout can be plumbed into the bath surround or wall-mounted, leaving the smooth shape of the tub uninterrupted.**
Far right **This classic plug is designed to fit neatly into the overflow outlet, which can be sited in the center or at the end of the bathtub.**

you. When you reach the corners, small sections of cut tile can be used to fill and finish—they are less obvious in a corner than in the middle of a room. You may also be reluctant to fit a shower cubicle or shower door to an enclosure against an uneven wall, but many manufacturers make doors that have generous rubber seals designed to accommodate a certain amount or irregularity.

Unless you are particularly good at home repairs, leave jobs such as putting up soap dishes, toothbrush holders, mirrors, and towel rods to a professional—especially if the surface to which these items must be attached is tiled or covered with a finish such as reinforced glass or marble. Drilling into tiles and other hard but brittle surfaces must be done with a carbide or similar implement to cope with the shiny or glazed finish and the hardness of the material. It may be very tricky and time-consuming to repair a cracked or scratched tile.

Water softeners

Although they are not new, water softeners are less bulky that they used to be. Whether or not you need one depends on where you live and what your water is like. Hard water is a product of high levels of calcium and magnesium salts dissolved as rain water filters through rocks. The salts themselves are invisible in water, but when they are heated, they appear as mineral scale. Hard water is not harmful to your health, but if deposits build up in pipes and hot-water radiators, they can reduce the efficiency of the heating system and lead to increased running costs. You will also need more soap, shampoo, and bubblebath to get a good lather if you live in a hard-water area.

A buildup of minerals in a shower head cuts down on its power and flow. Mineral deposits can also adversely affect enamel in a bathtub or shower pan and corrode the plating on faucets. Hard water can even destroy new products. For example, a heated brass towel rod can suffer dezincification as soon as hard water starts to flow through it, and in extreme cases can rot within six weeks of installation.

Water softeners are whole-houses systems that remove the minerals found in hard water. They not only make the water you use in the bathroom pleasanter and easier on the skin—

by a reverse osmosis filter—which uses the same technology that submarines use to filter salt from seawater. There are also a number of electronic devices that "condition" the water. They do not come into contact with the water itself, and do not therefore remove the hard salts, but they prevent them from forming a deposit. Radio waves are sometimes used to achieve the same effect.

people with eczema, for example, may find it gentler and less irritating—but they can also leave home-laundered clothes softer to the touch. A water softener may also help reduce wear and tear on a variety of equipment from toilets to dishwashers and washing machines.

Softeners are operated by an ion exchange system: the hard water is passed through a resin, initiating a process whereby hard calcium and magnesium ions are replaced with sodium ions, which come from common salt. The salt solution on which the system depends usually needs to be topped up with salt on a regular basis. Some of these devices can lead to high levels of sodium in the soft water, which makes it no good for drinking. To avoid this, some people connect softeners to hot-water pipes only. Alternatively, the sodium can be removed

2
styles and spaces

indulgent

streamlined

small spaces

showers and wet rooms

FASHIONS IN BATHROOMS CHANGE SLOWLY. STYLES IN FIXTURES ARE NOT AS

SHORT-LIVED AS FASHIONS IN CLOTHES BECAUSE BATHTUBS AND LAVS HAVE BEEN

CONSTRUCTED TO LAST FOR LONGER THAN A SINGLE SEASON, AND THEY ARE

EXPENSIVE TO REPLACE—INDEED, SOME CAST-IRON BATHTUBS DATING FROM

VICTORIAN TIMES ARE STILL IN REGULAR USE TODAY.

Since the 1930s, when bathrooms became a more widely integrated part of the house, there have been various fashionable phases, often lasting a decade or more. The trends have been especially noticeable in colors, but in general white has reigned supreme. With advances in technology and the introduction of new materials, shapes have become more unusual and adventurous; at the same time the classic Victorian rolltop tub with claw feet has not only survived, but has become increasingly popular.

As the bathroom changed from being a place purely for washing to a haven linked with relaxation, self-pampering, personal time, and privacy, decoration became more important and indulgent. In the 1950s and 1960s, bathroom fixtures were predominantly pastel—blue, turquoise, and primrose were among the sought-after shades. In the 1970s colours grew darker, and acrylic tubs, especially the luxurious corner bath, were the latest thing. The colors then were chocolate brown, pampas, and avocado.

In the mid-1980s a vogue for everything white began to gather pace, and bathroom styles became retrospective rather than forward-gazing. Victorian and Edwardian designs were reproduced and allied with modern plumbing technology, finishes, and mass production, making them more widely available, cost-effective, and reliable. White fixtures offered an unrivaled basis for the creation of any mood or

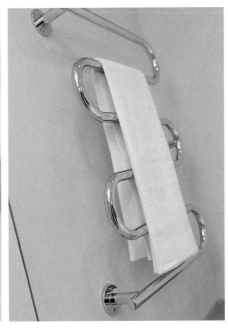

style. A bathroom with even the most daringly modern decoration is a suitable setting for a white rolltop bathtub, and a white toilet can be paired harmoniously with colors as startling as vermilion and as pale as pink. White is also timeless—it does not date in the same way as fashionably colored fixtures will.

In the 1990s designer names took on particular importance. Philippe Starck created his signature line for the Axor Hansgrohe group, and Dieter Sieger and Frank Huster brought the fashion for labels from the closet and the living room into the bathroom. Other trends, such as the interest in Feng Shui and Zen, have made their mark on the bathroom. Japanese-inspired wooden tubs can now be found in minimalist settings, and previously rare features such as Turkish-inspired steam rooms are now more commonplace.

New surface treatments have also provided a wider choice—ceramic tiles and vinyl wallpaper are no longer the only option. Concrete, once thought of as as cold and industrial, is tinted and finished to such a degree that it is not only acceptable but desirable indoors. Reinforced glass, now virtually unbreakable, is used for sinks as well as for large partitions and splash protection.

Having two or more bathrooms in a home offers great scope to the imagination, giving you the opportunity to decorate one, if not two, rooms in a scheme that is outrageous, indulgent, or fun.

indulgent

An indulgent bathroom is a place to wallow in a tubful of scented foam or stand in a shower with torrents of steamy warm water cascading over you —a haven where you can indulge yourself physically and mentally. To satisfy these needs, the room should be spacious and comfortable, with touches of luxury.

An indulgent bathroom can also be a place that lets you gratify your decorating fantasies. Public rooms, such as living and dining rooms, may be in the best understated taste, and a bedroom shared with a partner a decorative compromise, but if you are lucky enough to have more than one bathroom, or a separate shower room, you have the opportunity to be really adventurous.

Vivid red and pink clashing tiles; a mural; an underwater theme—you can let your imagination roam free. An indulgent bathroom could also be the place to use an expensive paper or fabric—something that would be inordinately extravagant in a bigger room, but is just affordable if you are buying no more than a single roll.

When planning an indulgent bathroom, make lists of colors you like, textures you enjoy, and images and themes—Indian, theatrical, or woodland, for example—that you find attractive. Then tear out pages of magazines featuring ideas, accessories, and rooms, and build up a reference file. You don't have to turn your bathroom into a replica or pastiche Indian temple; you can take elements of a pattern or a color reference, and use it in a subtle way that hints at the theme rather than

Right A grandly proportioned bathroom is the only appropriate setting for this Victorian-style basin with pillar pedestal, raised sculpted back, and wide surround.
Center **Placing a bathtub in the center of the room makes it the dominant feature and dissects the main floor space. This extravagantly luxurious oval bath—with its wood-paneled casing, broad upper rim, and plinth base—has been finished to resemble a piece of furniture.**

overstating it. The trend in this type of room is to take the best from the past and combine it with complementary examples of modern design. A classic rolltop bathtub fitted with a modern lever faucet reflects a successful blend of old and new, as does a modern tub with traditional crosshead faucets. If you favor the mix-and-match approach, try to keep the fixtures and their shapes uniform. For example, select either chrome or brass faucets and spouts rather than combining the two colors and types of finish, and for the bathtub, bidet, toilet and sink, choose shapes that are either rounded or angular, not both.

Comfort, convenience, and luxury

The indulgent bathroom is a place to pamper your mind and body in serene and relaxing surroundings. Some people enjoy a long deep bath by candlelight with music playing and thick furry towels warming on a

Below left **A double sink unit has been installed under a graceful arch. The wall behind is mirrored, with the glass cut to accentuate the architectural shape, and slim mirror panels have been added at the sides. There is ample storage under the sinks and in rows of small drawers beside the main cabinets.**

Above **Beaded lampshades on elaborate wall-mounted lights and a beaded fringe along the front edge of the sink complement an ornate mirror and a generously draped curtain. This is a decorative style that needs to be viewed and enjoyed at leisure; it is not for the purely functional bathroom.**

heated rod ready to envelop them when they step out of the water. It may add to the pleasure to have comfortable objects in the room—a chair or chaise longue where the bather can lie and recover, wrapped in a deep-pile dressing gown, with a stack of magazines to read and maybe something to eat and drink.

An air of opulence can be achieved by adding a thick absorbent cotton mat over a parquet floor, pots of plants or flowers to provide color and interest, and underfloor heating to guarantee that even a mosaic tile or stone surface is comfortable to stand on and that no stepping-stone

surface will preserve your modesty while allowing light into the room and giving a view of the sky in the upper half. Remember that if a light is turned on inside the room, your outline will be silhouetted against the frosted glass—so for morning and evening bathing in winter, you may need the additional shield of a blind or curtain.

An indulgent bathroom may also be reflected in the quality, style, and type of its fixtures. A rolltop tub plumbed into the center of a room gives an air of splendor because the bathtub is the focal point of the room and takes up more space than necessary. While retaining the classic shape and

Organic tactile surfaces such as wood, stone, plaster, and glass can give a bathroom a human touch—an earthiness that is in strong contrast with the fast-moving, hi-tech world outside.

action from mat to mat is required to cross the floor. The arrangement of storage and shelves, soap trays, and similar holders in the bathroom should be carefully thought out to enhance the sense of relaxation. It is enjoyable to be able to put out your hand and find a warm dry towel, the bottle of shampoo, a sponge, or whatever it may be, without having to get out of the bathtub and plod dripping across the floor. Having things at hand may extend to touch-sensitive remote-control panels that allow you to adjust the pressure of the jets in a spa bath or the temperature of the water with the mere touch of a fingertip. Automatic devices can be programmed to fill the bathtub or turn on the shower with water at a preset temperature.

When it comes to being indulgent, some people find that less is more and that serenity lies in simplicity and understated elegance. The eyes and mind can be soothed by the graphic lines and play of light on a glass sink or the view of the backyard or treetops from the bathroom window. If you are an adherent of this philosophy, then the few items you have in a bathroom can be of very good quality because you won't need to set aside money for additional decoration or accessories.

Light is an important factor in creating the right ambience. It is satisfying to be able to take a bath in daylight and stare out of the window without being seen. In many modern bathrooms, such a sense of privacy can be achieved by installing a skylight. This means the bather can contemplate clouds, treetops and birds in flight as though through a huge telescope, but without the danger of becoming a neighborhood spectacle. If an overhead window is not feasible, you could put frosted glass into the lower half of a conventional wall-sited window. The opaque

white-enameled finish, the rolltop tub can be given elaborate finishing touches such as gilded claw feet or an interesting paint finish on the exposed sides. Reproduction Victorian- and Edwardian-style lavs often have decorative finishes and integral features such as raised surrounds that wrap around the back of the basin and gradually taper down the sides, and soap recesses sculpted to resemble shells.

Large double-ended bathtubs also need space. If the tub is for shared bathing, the plug and overflow should be located in the middle so that no one has to sit on the uncomfortable bit. Wall-mounted faucets in the center of the side of the bath also avoid the crick in the neck that can be inflicted by trying to keep the spout out of your ear on one side and the faucets from digging into your back on the other.

Corner bathtubs, which were once thought the height of luxury, are now commonplace. They can be useful in an awkwardly shaped bathroom where the siting of the door and windows prevents the use of a single long wall to rest the tub against. Recent designs have favored more angular shapes and can be based on a diamond rather than an oval inner recess. Some manufacturers include a seat area, which can be useful if you simply want to rinse your feet or give children somewhere to sit while they are being showered or washed. If showering is your preferred

This sculptural tub has been designed with a stepped, curved wall to contain spray from the two showers—one on a flexible hose, the other on a rigid arm above the center of the tub. Niches have been recessed into the corner to hold shower gels or bath preparations.

Far left **The delicate wrought-iron and glass dressing table and chair provide the perfect place to apply cosmetics and style hair in this bathroom that doubles as a dressing room. The mirrors are placed so they can be used while sitting or standing, and make use of the ample natural light.**

Left **Perfumes are best stored away from direct light since the sun can cause the scent to turn, and glass bottles are best kept out of the bathroom in case they fall against a hard surface and break.**

method of washing, you may choose an extra-large shower head that gives a wider-than-average spray, a shower with an adjustable head that offers a choice of spray types from needle-fine to massage, or a multijet shower cubicle where jets positioned at different heights give you an all-round wash.

Architectural details can add to the overall indulgent appearance of a bathroom. An archway or recess can be accented with color or a mirror, or even used as a niche into which a shower or a sink and bidet can be installed. Door frames and baseboards can also be highlighted with a different shade of paint from the walls. Another option is to create architectural features. For example, you could construct a solid curved bench as part of the wall by the shower. The bench will in itself add a pleasing and interesting shape to the room, but it may also be used to conceal pipes and provide a place to lay towels or clothes ready for when you emerge from the shower.

A window seat is another useful feature. The hinged top can be padded with a simple cushion, and the boxed base provides storage space for bulky things such as toilet paper or detergents and cleaning solutions.

Colors and materials

Color is important in creating the right mood in a bathroom. In addition to the natural palette of muted earthy colors such as cream, beige, soft greens, and browns, which can have very relaxing and calming effects, there are other shades that can be used to create different

Far left **Installing a bath and shower in separate areas of the same room gives plenty of space for both bathing and showering. Recessed up- and downlighters offer illumination that can be varied to suit the mood— either full-on for a brisk morning shower or more subdued for a leisurely soak. Efficient drainage is provided by a central grille set directly under the shower head.**
Left **Lining the edge of this bath with a mirrored surround is a simple way to make a small bathroom seem larger. It also helps to reflect light, making a dark or windowless room appear lighter.**

moods in various lights. Yellow can be pale and refreshing in the morning daylight, but warm and golden in subdued light or candlelight. A single wall of red can bring color and interest to a room, being bright and vibrant in the daytime but rich and enveloping in artificial light—but be cautious about painting all the walls in a small bathroom with a strong red because the result may be overpowering and claustrophobic. Blue is a watery color that can be refreshing first thing in the morning, but in a dim light will contribute toward creating a restful and peaceful atmosphere.

Some people find that pattern in a bathroom can be distracting or overwhelming, but there are subtle ways of using it to add unobtrusive interest and a variation of color. For example, different shades of mosaic tile can be used, tone on tone, to create the effect of a wash of color across a room, or from the floor to the ceiling, getting gradually lighter toward the ceiling as though the observer were looking up at the sky from under the sea.

A couple of lines of contrasting colors of tile can create a mock dado effect and give definition to the space or delineate different areas in the room such as the shower, bathtub and washbasin. Classic patterns such as the geometric Greek key or Moorish crenellation will give a touch of exoticism without being overpowering.

Fabric is generally best kept to a minimum in a bathroom, but it may be used sparingly to add touches of color and pattern. Decorative shower curtains can be made by lining a glamorous, untreated exterior fabric with a plain plastic shower curtain. For example, a length or remnant of rich purple velvet could be lined with a purchased shower curtain and hung over the tub. When someone is using the shower, the inner plastic curtain should be tucked inside the edge of the bathtub to contain splashes and the velvet left hanging over the outer edge so the

Above and right **Overflow outlets are plumbed through to the main waste pipe, which runs down the back of the basin and takes water from the main plug. Overflows are an important means of preventing flooding in both the basin and the bath. if the taps are left on by mistake, or if the bath is overfilled and runs over when the bather gets in, the overflow outlet can come to the rescue.**

reverse side of the velvet is protected by the other curtain. This sort of two-layer curtain could also be used as a way of softening the angular lines of the bathtub and adding a touch of decadence.

Organic tactile surfaces such as wood, stone, plaster, and glass give a human touch—an earthiness that is in strong contrast with the fast-moving, hi-tech world outside. Marble, limestone, granite, and soapstone are good materials for floors and surfaces because they are impervious to water and can be cut into relatively thin tiles and slabs so the accumulated weight does not put a heavy burden on beams or boards.

Tongue-and-groove wood floors can create an intimate atmosphere in a large room, but may be overpowering and intrusive in a small room. Tongue-and-groove flooring can also create different moods: if it is

Top left **A floral design fired into the glaze makes this Victorian-style sink attractive as well as durable.**
Far left **The indulgent bathroom is the opposite of austere—an ornate candlestick or a fine old toy can be part of the decorative scheme.**
Left **Unusual fixtures such as this soap and jar holder may be found in antique stores and flea markets and can be restored.**
Below left **Keep potions, lotions, and cotton balls in containers to avoid mess.**
Right **A rolltop bathtub takes pride of place in the period-style bathroom. The simple paneling, the figurative plaster roundel, and the antique metal sink and stand add a few touches of luxury.**

painted in pale flat colors such as powder blue and stone, it can be reminiscent of the chic shoreline residences of New England around Nantucket and Cape Cod; in bright blue or red striped with white, it is more likely to give the impression of a Coney Island beach theme; in subtle washes of green or lavender, the flooring may have overtones of Scandinavian interiors.

Concrete can be tinted and mixed with various resins to give a variety of appearances, but make sure the finish is smooth. Concrete with sharp peaks could graze your skin, and a roughly textured wall may trap moisture in small pockets, which can linger and become damp-smelling—and even encourage mold in a poorly ventilated room.

Right and far right **Copper is a good conductor of heat— so a copper bathtub will warm through quickly, but it is advisable to protect it with a seal. A copper tub must be well maintained to prevent residue water from causing a verdigris stain. This deep, Empire-style bathtub has centrally located faucets and drain so the bather may choose at which end to recline.**

Various unusual materials have been used to create bathtubs, among them glass, stone, and copper. These are rare, usually custom-made, and therefore expensive, and they may need, on account of their weight, to be sited on a ground floor or one that has been specially reinforced. Copper and similar unenameled metal tubs require specialized cleaning, and wooden tubs, such as the Japanese-style bath that has become popular, are not suitable for use with detergents or certain soaps, whose cleaning and grease-cutting qualities will destroy the wood's natural oil. Some wooden tubs also need to be kept constantly moist—otherwise, the wood will dry out and shrink, and may split.

Spas and whirlpool baths

In a spa bath air is pumped into the tub through small jets arranged inside its base; when the tub is full, the jets of air send streams of bubbles rippling through the water. The bubbling effect creates a sparkling sensation on the

skin, which is said to benefit blood circulation. Whirlpool baths generally work by recirculating the bath water, often through adjustable jets, allowing you to target particular areas of the body. They tend to have more powerful jets than a spa bath. A combination whirlpool-and-spa bath pumps a mixture of water and air into the tub. Designs at the top end of the line have a control that allows you to adjust the strength from a relaxing bath with a gentle ripple to a full-scale "massage" treatment. Some types also have built-in heaters to prevent the water from cooling while it is bubbling.

Many of the more expensive spa baths have built-in head and arm rests to support the bather comfortably. Underwater lighting, music systems, and waterproof remote-control panels are also available for those who wish to pay for them. For pure indulgence there is the

Above **Although the black and white minimalist decoration could have given this bathroom a cold character, the warm wood flooring with black diamond inset—which complements the color on the side of the rolltop tub—adds warmth and comfort. Glass shelves provide useful storage and display space, but because they are transparent they do not clutter up the wall.**

Far left **Mirror is a useful waterproof finish that can also be used as a facing on a cabinet or a bulky unit, where its effect will be to make the object less dominant.**

Left **Glass blocks are also bathroom-friendly and have the advantage of allowing light to pass through while partially obscuring the view. Their overall weight can be very heavy, so they need careful installation.**

Below **Wood is another material that is suitable for a bathroom—or, as shown here, in a sauna—but make sure the wood you choose is well seasoned and finished specifically for use in a bathroom.**

heat, which is effective in cleansing the skin pores and encouraging a good, deep sweat. The warmth of the steam is also said to increase blood flow. But anyone with breathing difficulties, people with heart conditions, and pregnant women should consult their doctor before entering a steam cabinet. The temperature of the steam needs careful regulation, because steam stores and conducts heat more effectively than air and can rise to temperatures higher than those reached by boiling water.

All you need to make a steam room is a fully enclosed space such as a pod or capsule shower, or a purpose-built shower enclosure that is extended to the ceiling and has built-in areas over the door and side panels. The steam generator, which resembles a big kettle, is kept outside the cabinet and can be plumbed in through a small opening in the wall or panel. The steam is pumped in through a nozzle until it gradually fills the space. Before installing a steam generator, check with the manufacturer of the shower cabinet or enclosure that the glass and rubber seals on the doors and supports are compatible with this sort of use.

Hydrosonic system by Teuco, which has whirlpool jets with ultrasound waves, that provide a deep muscle massage. This sort of treatment would be especially beneficial for people who feel stiff after long and frequent bursts of sport, gardening, or golf, but for most of us the conventional spa or whirlpool is enough.

If you intend to have a spa or whirlpool system installed in an existing bathtub, the installation should be done by a professional because it will require electrical wiring work, and adjustments may be necessary to suit the size and volume of your bath. Whatever type of spa or whirlpool bath you possess, it is advisable periodically to run a disinfectant through the system to prevent the buildup of bacteria and to give the interior pipes a thorough cleaning.

Before using bubblebath or other bath preparations in a whirlpool or spa system, check with the supplier that there is no danger that they could damage the pump mechanism or reduce effectiveness. You should also avoid using too much bubblebath because the aerating quality of such preparations can make the soapsuds overactive.

Saunas and steam rooms

Saunas are often sold as wooden cabinets, about the size of a small garden shed. Inside the cabinet are usually two rows of built-in benches or shelves to sit on—one at a lower, cooler level, the other at the higher, hotter position. Saunas encourage sweating and have a cleansing effect, but the atmosphere is drier than in a steam room, which can be awkward for people with breathing problems or for wearers of contact lenses.

Steam rooms are taking over the luxury end of the market that was once dominated by spas and whirlpools. The steam room gives a wet

streamlined

The streamlined bathroom is primarily a place for quick washing and grooming. It is not, on the face of it, somewhere to linger. A bathroom of this type is defined by form and function; it is seen at its best first thing in the morning when the alarm clock sounds and you head straight for the shower, then over to the sink and back to the bedroom to get dressed. Everything in the room is designed to aid speed and efficiency.

The layout of the streamlined bathroom should be carefully planned, especially if two people are likely to be using the room at the same time. For example, it may make sense to arrange the fixtures and items of furniture in a linear fashion to allow enough space for one person to pass comfortably by the other. Before reaching any decisions, try to visualize the probable morning routine and walk through the scene in an imaginary bathroom to determine where the various objects should be positioned for maximum efficiency and ease of use.

Many manufacturers of ceramic and pressed steel bathroom fixtures have lines with a contemporary edge that are styled to meet these requirements. Designers such as Dieter Sieger, Frank Huster, and Philippe Starck have also brought their ideas and knowledge to bear on the development of a wider choice of products.

Computerized design and the availability of new materials have given manufacturers the ability to satisfy more specific needs. For example, there are shallow oblong sinks that are perfect for brushing teeth and washing hands. This type of sink does not require much water to fill and fits neatly into a narrow vanity unit or onto a benchlike unit—it may be all that is needed if you wash from head to toe in the shower and use an electric razor for shaving (if applicable). Shower stalls also come in a wide variety of styles and finishes. Sculpted styles include a design made from overlapping curves, which has no doors to negotiate nor curtains to cling clammily to your warm wet skin. You simply walk in around the bend of the first curve, which is overlapped by the curve of the second, creating an enclosed pod. An alternative is a wet room—a waterproof showering area in which it doesn't matter where the spray flies.

The bathtub is usually a secondary element in this type of bathroom, but there are styles that have been designed to be linear rather than rounded, and where the inside is molded in the shape of a figure-eight, so a bath uses less water and provides a soak but within a more confined space than the oval corner tub or classic rolltop. The single-ended tub with a sloping incline at only one end is also suitable for a streamlined bathroom. As is the case

Far left **More of a washing shelf than a sink, this fixture is long enough to allow two people to wash at the same time, but has been devised as a single length with a central drain. Its simple linear shape and functional form make it a strong feature in a streamlined bathroom.**
Left and below **Streamlined design does not mean that the space has to be cold, hard, and unattractive.**

with many contemporary kitchen features, the inspiration for the design of some of these bathroom fixtures springs from utilitarian settings such as hospitals.

Where the home kitchen has taken its style from the professional restaurant or hotel kitchen, the streamlined bathroom has drawn on features found in institutions such as prisons, factories, and military barracks. These apparently unpromising sources use items of stainless-steel equipment that are functional, often minimally styled, and simply finished—exactly the qualities that appeal to the designers of modern bathrooms.

The idea of a stainless-steel bathroom may seem cold and hard, but as long as the room is adequately heated, there is no reason why it should be any colder or harder than cast iron or enameled steel. Some custom-made stainless-steel bathtubs are double-skinned so the air between the two layers acts as insulation against heat loss. The double thickness also gives the tub a more solid appearance than would otherwise be the case—the steel

can be rolled in a slim sheet that is perfectly viable but may appear rather thin and insubstantial. Stainless-steel tubs often come in smooth, sculpted shapes, and some manufacturers offer a choice between a highly polished "mirror" surface and a more muted "burnished" version. Their neat, uncluttered lines make stainless-steel fixtures easy to clean, but non-abrasive cream or spray cleaner may be needed to prevent scratching.

Traditional faucets and spouts can complement modern fixtures but, if you are seeking speed and efficiency, some of the more recent innovations are worth considering. One of the more unobtrusive designs is Hansgrohe's combined overflow and faucet in one minimalist unit with a side lever to open the waste. Grohtec's Special Fittings line was originally designed for commercial use, but is ideal for the hi-tech bathroom and can now be installed in home settings. The fixture is a single spout with an infrared electronic sensor; water flows—at a pre-determined temperature—only when the user's hands are

Below left, below and right
In addition to well-designed storage space, the shower, sinks and toilet are generally more important than the tub in this style of bathroom. The functional elements may be grouped together for ease of access, and the tub put at the far side of the room—becoming in effect a separate entity, to be used at another time. In this example, disk-shaped hot and cold knobs have been inserted into the bath deck, so that they remain within easy reach without interrupting the line of the broad oval rim.

underneath the electronic sensing spot. Armitage Shanks's Sensorflow is another electronic system capable of detecting whether or not hands are present.

Lever faucets are also appropriate in the streamlined bathroom. The single-lever mixer is a practical, elegant design that does away with the clutter of separate knobs. The lever is simply moved from the cold to the hot end of the spectrum until the right temperature is reached, and water flows through a single spout. Some lever faucets come with a safety stop that controls access to the hot end of the lever's sweep, thereby preventing scalds.

If the streamlined bathroom is meant to be a relaxing venue, the lighting arrangement is important. The lights should be wired on two circuits, with dimmer switches, so for the all-action morning routine the lights can be on full, targeting areas such as the sinks and shower. In the evening, or at a quieter time of the day, the main over-sink lights can be dimmed or turned off, leaving a soft halo of light on the second circuit around the periphery

Right and far right **This single, custom-made metal sink is shallow compared with the traditional ceramic style, but the amount of water it holds is more than adequate for brushing teeth and washing hands and faces. Specialized cream cleaners should be used on this type of surface; those with an abrasive content may scratch or mark the metal.** Above **The metallic theme is taken through to the toilet, which is wall-hung with the tank concealed behind the wall.**

Left **A Philippe Starck mono sink faucet combines knob and spout in a single unit. The featherlike lever on top controls the flow and temperature of water. The lever is rounded and slightly curved, which makes it easy to hold and maneuver, even with wet hands.**

Below **This water spout is plumbed directly into the floor so that it arches neatly over the side of the bath.**

Top right **The faucet is integral to the slim tubular support on which this glass sink is mounted. The water flow and temperature is selected by twisting the upper section of the pillar, which is a movable disk.**

Center right **A plain spout is attached directly to the wall.**

Far right **Simple stylized levers instead of knobs are used to supply hot and cold water to a mixer spout.**

of the room. Another option is to direct a couple of dimmed lights onto the bathtub and extinguish the other circuit, leaving the rest of the room in darkness. Burning incense will add a subtle scent to the air, and candles and deep-pile towels can also be put to good use.

Mirrors are another important element of the streamlined bathroom. The mirror behind the sink should be not only functional, but also aesthetically pleasing. There is no point in having a badly illuminated, small mirror that requires you to stretch over the sink and allows you to glimpse only a small part of yourself at one time. One option is to mirror the whole area behind the sink. This can be done with a single large sheet of mirror or a grid of mirror tiles.

The mirror's glass facing is waterproof and will serve as easy-to-clean splash protection as well as providing an ample viewing area. If you choose this option, put a generous line of sealant or caulk or some other filling device between the mirror and the sink or any supporting unit; otherwise, water may seep behind the mirror and damage the silvered backing. In a steamy bathroom, water will condense when it comes into contact with the coolness of the mirror and the drops of water will trickle down the surface and seep through cracks or seams at its base.

If you prefer a mirror for individual use, consider the classic Eileen Gray design that has a small mirror on an adjustable arm in front of the large one. Modern copies can be found, and the small mirror is usually a magnifier, which is perfect for close scrutiny. Double-sided magnifying mirrors are available on extendable metal arms that can be pulled forward and pressed back flat against the wall surface as required. This type of mirror is useful for shaving, applying make-up, or inserting contact lenses.

A casual display or arrangement of some natural objects can prevent a streamlined room from looking too clinical. For example, a glass or stone bowl or a simple basket filled with natural sponges, a couple of loofahs, and a Japanese lather brush would create an effect that is both decorative and appropriate to the setting. If you are concerned to keep cleaning simple, avoid dust-gathering items such as bowls of potpourri, sample soaps and miniature shampoo bottles from hotels, and frilly, floral-printed fabric covers for tissue boxes and toilet paper.

If a streamlined bathroom opens directly into another room, such as a bedroom or dressing room, you may wish to disguise the fixtures to give the impression that the bathroom is a continuation of the other room. One way to do this is to create a wall or doors behind which a

Above **By varying the levels in a room, you can create the illusion of spaciousness. This bathroom has steps leading up to a raised level from which the sunken bath can be reached.**
Above right and right **The bidet and toilet have been hung onto the side of the bathtub—a practical arrangement that means all the wastepipes can be ducted away from the same area and concealed behind a single façade. The shower is located behind a simple reinforced glass panel. Folding doors between the bedroom and bathroom can be closed to create privacy in either area—or opened to provide a generous vista.**

Right **Cabinet space below a sink is useful because it means you can keep the toiletries you need close at hand and put them away easily when they are no longer needed. This cone-shaped unit has been fashioned in a modern style from a traditional material.**

shower and a sink, for example, are hidden. In such situations the cabinets that enclose the fixtures should have extractor fans to expel moisture and steam. Some options for creating streamlined bathrooms in small spaces are examined in the next section, pages 68–79.

Colors and materials

Although the streamlined bathroom is often conceived as an unfussy, somewhat austere area, you can introduce elements of modern glamour that harmonize with its practical character. White is a favorite color for this room because it gives a fresh, clean, simple appearance, but be careful to make sure the bathroom does not take on a cold and institutional appearance. Touches of color can soften the strictness and make the place warmer and more inviting, but try to restrict the scheme you use to one main color and a contrasting one or to two or three shades of the same color.

A soft wash of an earthy tone—such as a hint of green or beige—will reduce the austerity of a predominantly white room. If there are plenty of steel or chrome surfaces in the room, you may discover that paints and fabrics with blue or turquoise overtones only enhance the impression of coolness, but if the blue is mixed with a little pink, creating a shade that is closer to lavender, a warmer effect will be achieved.

Acid colors such as citrus yellow and fluorescent lime can be effective with white and steel, and give a bright, zesty edge to a color scheme. Strong and fashionable colors of this type should be used sparingly and preferably as paint or in an accessory so when the trend passes, or you tire of the color, it can be removed easily. If you use such a color in tiles or another more permanent feature, it will be messy, expensive, and time-consuming to replace.

Window treatments can be used to add color and interest. Roll-up shades made with a finely punched or perforated random design will let light filter through and create patterns on the walls and floors. A tone-on-tone striped fabric can also be used as a shade and will provide pattern and a variety of shades of a single color. Fine-slat louver blinds come in a wide choice of colors and unusual finishes, including metallic, and have a businesslike appearance.

The floor surface in a streamlined bathroom should be waterproof and easy to wipe down; underfloor heating could do away with the need for slippers, making it an

even simpler place to walk into and use. If the room has minimal decoration, the floor may be a place to introduce a little color, texture, or pattern. There are many modern floor tiles that have specks of reflective material in them, giving the impression that they contain a sprinkling of gold, silver, or titanium.

One flooring option for this type of bathroom is textured rubber—another idea that has its roots in industrial warehouses and hospitals. Rubber flooring is hardwearing and has a warmer feel underfoot than unheated stone and ceramic surfaces; it can also provide a certain level of heat and sound insulation.

Some people prefer a good-quality, vinyl-tile copy of marble, granite, or slate flooring because the imitation is warmer, softer and, in most cases, cheaper than the real thing. Laminate floors that resemble wood—with finishes ranging from parquet to "driftwood"—are also worth considering for a heavily used bathroom, because thet can be easily wiped clean of splashes without the hazard of marking or staining that comes with a genuine wood floor.

On shiny floor surfaces such as marble or polished ceramic tiles always use nonslip bathmats. A bathroom is full of hard surfaces, and to slip and fall against one could be painful. Many bathmats are sold with a light rubber mesh on the back that grips the floor surface, or you can buy a double-sided grip backing that can be attached to the mat and the floor, but as bathmats need regular machine-washing, it is advisable to buy one that has an integral back.

Cork and wooden mats are a good alternative to a cotton or fabric mat, although you need to be sure the cork has been sealed—or it will absorb water and gradually disintegrate. Wooden mats or duckboards are made from lengths of wood secured over a frame, rather like decking found outdoors. These boards mean the water can drip from you onto the floor rather than absorbing the moisture, so they should be used only on waterproof flooring.

Surfaces and storage

To maintain the integrity of the streamlined look, try to keep surfaces uncluttered. A cabinet directly beside the sink, with a door opening away from you, provides easily accessible storage for most of the items that commonly accumulate around the sink or on the shelf above it.

The surfaces in a bathroom look best when they are clean. Products such as toothpaste and shaving gel tend to leave opaque marks and residues, and hairs may accumulate on the shelf in front of the mirror and in the drain, so for easy cleaning it is advisable to keep the skin, bathtub, and shower areas free of bottles and cosmetic products. The more laborious option is to pick up the bottles and tubes, move them, do the cleaning, and then replace them.

Many beauty preparations and products based on liquid soap are greasy and prone to leaking, so you may choose to line the shelves on which they are stored with an easily removable rubber mat that can be taken out and showered clean. Reinforced-glass shelves and ceramic tiles are equally easy to clean with a damp cloth. Some people

Below **Glass and mirror are light and reflective surfaces that feel and look clean and fresh. Tempered and reinforced versions are available for safe use on walls and surfaces such as sink units. Glass can also be molded to form sinks and even bathtubs, but these surfaces should be kept clean because smears and water stains will make them less attractive.**

Above **The molded sink and surrounding area eliminates all the seams and cracks that can harbor germs or bits of fluff and grime. This sink will need to be wiped often, and even polished, to avoid marks from toothpaste and soap scum.**

Top right **Decant bath and shampoo products into sturdy, unbreakable metal or plastic containers.**

Below right **A functional hook for towels or robes.**

use a narrow terrycloth mat, a small hand towel, or a couple of washcloths as shelf liners. The terrycloth absorbs the drips and moisture that may have covered the bottles in the shower or during use. When the mat gets stained or marked, it can easily be taken away and washed or replaced with another.

To keep the number of bottles and jars in your bathroom to a minimum, be disciplined about finishing one bottle before opening another. If you stop using a product or find that one doesn't suit you, throw it away there and then. Don't store things at the back of a shelf or cabinet thinking that they will come in handy some time—almost invariably they simply gather dust until you move or redecorate the room. In addition to the regularly used products that need to be within easy reach, spare items can also be kept in the bathroom if there is enough space. Then, if you run out of something while having a bath, it will save you having to get dry, find a bathrobe, and go looking for it elsewhere in your home. Ideally, there should be storage space for spare toilet paper, cotton balls, facial tissues, toothpaste, soap, shampoo, and shower gels. Another type of storage to

In addition to being a place for bathing, the bathroom is often where you undress, so it is a sensible place to have a laundry bag, sack, or basket. For a bachelor pad, a calico or linen bag hanging on a peg behind a door may be enough, but for a household of two or more people, especialy those with young children, a larger receptacle will be required. In a streamlined bathroom the container could be a slick chrome pedal

Equipment found in prisons, factories, and military barracks is functional, often minimally styled, and simply finished—exactly the qualities that appeal to modern bathroom designers.

This wet room has plastered walls with a soft warm terracotta coloring that contrasts with the smoothly painted wall outside. The floor, seen in detail below, is made from stone slabs that are placed slightly apart so that the water runs down between them and into a central drain below.

consider in a streamlined bathroom is hanging space for robes, towels in use, and clothes that have been taken off or are waiting to be put on. Towels should be hung on a rod to dry; if left damp and crumpled, they may begin to smell musty.

A chair, window seat, or the top of a laundry basket are frequently used to lay clothes on, but an interesting alternative is the Shaker peg rail, which—though neither hi-tech nor a modern piece of design—provides an eminently efficient hanging system.

A Shaker peg rail, or a modern interpretation with metal hooks or horn-shaped pegs, can be screwed along the wall above head height so it does not impede movement or cause things to catch on it. The back board can be painted to match the wall so that it almost disappears—or, if you want to make it a prominent feature, paint it in a contrasting shade. The pegs can be used for hanging up all sorts of things such as clothes and towels, but in the streamlined bathroom this should be done with restraint—otherwise, the peg rail could come to resemble a messy clothesline.

Open shelving can be an attractive feature in a bathroom, but in this style of room the objects on display should be uniform or of similar colors and shapes. They should also be able to tolerate a damp and steamy atmosphere. A pile of neatly folded towels in a single color is useful as well as attractive—the towels will be used, washed, and replaced, so there is no need to worry about their becoming damp or moldy, or collecting dust.

Glass shelves are inconspicuous and light, easy to clean, and timeless, but, for safety, they must be laminated or made of a reinforced material. Barely visible plexiglass has a similar appearance to glass and is safer because it is virtually unbreakable, but it can become cloudy from numerous little scratches on the surface and should be cleaned only with the specialized products recommended by the manufacturer.

can, perhaps lined with a removable and washable cloth inner bag that can be easily lifted out when full and transported to the washing machine. Wicker baskets have long been popular, especially the style known as the Ali Baba, but the outer edges of the wicker may be rough and can snag pantyhose and other fine materials.

Opaque, lightweight plastic cans in interesting colors are also available—they have the advantage of being easily cleaned and dried should any wet clothes be dropped inside them or water splashed on the outside when someone is using the bathroom.

small spaces

A combination of improved plumbing and specially designed fixtures means that smaller and smaller areas, including niches that were once dismissed as dead spaces, are now being utilized to make bathrooms. Broom closets—those all-important glory holes under the stairs where stacks of old magazines lurk—are just the sort of places that are increasingly likely to be transformed into a shower, or bathroom.

A glance at the broom closet would probably leave you with the impression that there is no way in which a viable bathroom could be installed in such a small space—there would be hardly enough room to stretch out a towel and dry yourself, let alone to accommodate bulky equipment. But you may be surprised to discover how, with careful planning and the selection of well-designed fixtures, it is possible to create a bathroom or half-bath in the most apparently unpromising places.

To gather some ideas, consider and study other small spaces containing bathroom fixtures. For example, many hotel baths are compact but luxurious. A yacht's "head" is likely to have a small countersunk sink with a lid that can be closed to make a useful surface, as well as a shower installed over a removable section of wooden flooring that hides a shower pan.

In aircraft, the necessary facilities are crammed into a tiny space—but they nevertheless serve the purpose they were designed for, even in almost constant use thousands of feet up in the sky.

Different types of use

When you have found your space, you must decide what exactly you need—a small main bathroom, connecting or otherwise, an ancillary bathroom, or a half-bath.

Even if there is no overriding need for extra facilities in your home, using a small space to create an additional bathroom can bring bonuses. For example, guests who stay overnight or for a weekend will enjoy having their own bathroom. It will make them less self-conscious about leaving their personal belongings lying around, and when they waken in the morning they will not feel under pressure to spend as little time as possible getting

Opposite page **A linear arrangement of fixtures often makes the best use of space in a narrow bathroom. Here the tub is placed at the far end of the room. At its foot is one of a pair of sinks mounted on a simple stone base, and beside it stand a shower with clear glass walls, which contain the spray without restricting** the view. **On the near side of the shower are a toilet and the second sink. The passageway of narrow-slat wooden decking provides a slip-proof floor covering that is also warm under bare feet.**

Left and below **The wall beside this tub is glass, which can be left unlit and transparent with a view through to the bedroom,** making the space seem larger and allowing extra light to shine through. The glazed panel incorporates an interlay that becomes opaque at the flick of an electrical switch, giving privacy to anyone using the bathroom. Because the edge of the tub can be seen from the bedroom, it is kept clear of bottles and soap.

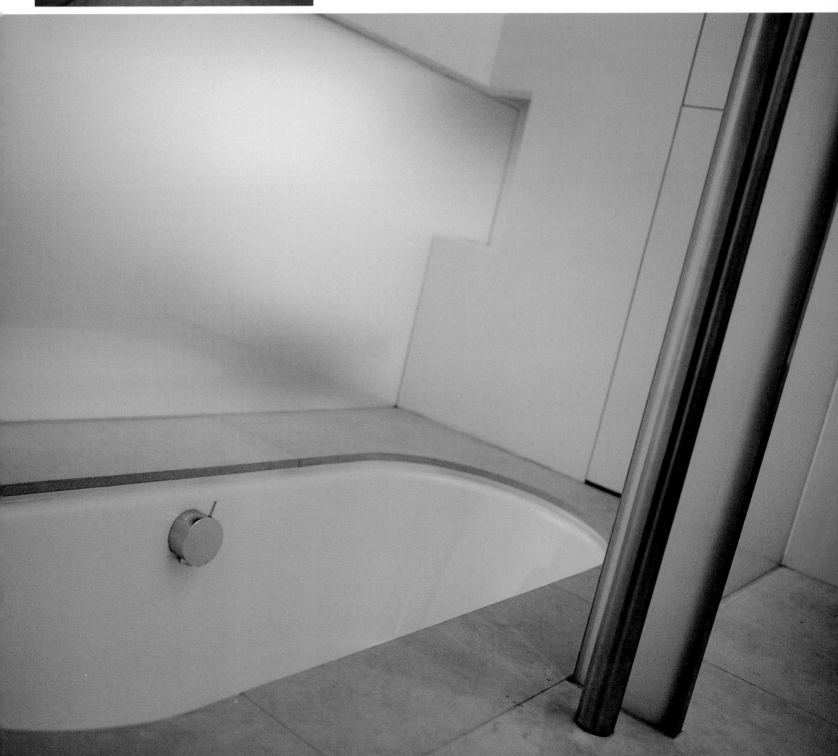

ready for the day ahead while a line forms on the other side of the door. Installing an extra bathroom may also increase the value of your home and, when you come to sell, could give your property an edge over similar properties on the market.

The small main bathroom found in a modern apartment or studio in a converted building is often the only enclosed space and may be located in a space that was never intended to be a bathroom. Its position may have been dictated by the way in which the house or building was divided into apartments—to give easy access to pipework or for some other practical rather than aesthetic reason.

But, as the saying goes, small can be beautiful. Whatever your raw material, it is well worth spending time on the research and planning for this type of room, and discussing your ideas with other people. A sheet of graph paper marked with the dimensions of the space, and squares of paper cut out to the size and shape of the fixtures, are very useful tools if you want to examine the various options. Move the larger pieces around until you find areas where there is enough wall space to support them, then try to squeeze in the ancillary equipment around them.

Below **An uncomplicated, cabinetlike shower enclosure and a narrow, double trough sink provide adequate facilities for washing and occupy a minimal amount of space.**

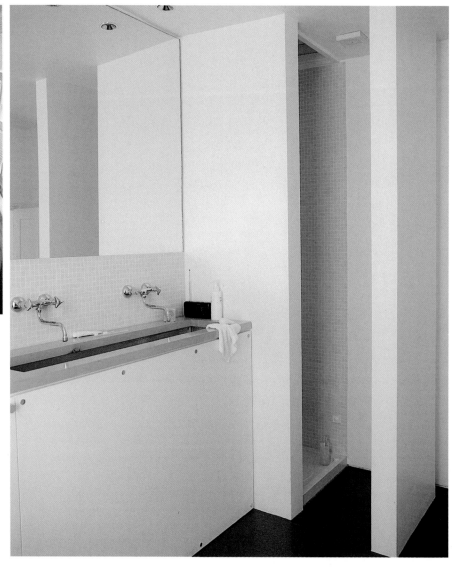

Left and top **This bathroom follows a linear design. The tub has been fitted into an area with restricted head room—which is acceptable because the tub is intended purely for sitting or lying in. The shower, lined with small mosaic tiles, has been plumbed in at the other end of the room, where the walls reach full head height.**

Above **A shower has been fitted in behind the sink by using a gently curving wall and a sink specifically designed to fit into a corner. Glass bricks allow a good flow of natural light into both the shower and the bathroom. The blue mosaic tiles add to the impression of light and freshness, which is important in a small space.**

A secondary bathroom is often installed to relieve demand on the main bathroom. When planning such a room, you need to determine its main function. Will it be at its busiest when the children are getting ready for school? Do the people in your household prefer taking baths or showers? If you simply need a back-up bathroom for quick washing, do not try to squeeze in a tub—simply plumb in a shower and make more practical use of the remaining space.

If the small additional bathroom is intended to be a place where you can lock yourself away in a soapy bath for relaxation while the main bathroom bears the brunt of the family wear and tear, then you could choose a tub with a hand-held shower as part of the fixture, or perhaps an over-bath shower with a curtain rather than a solid panel.

Depending on the dimensions of the room and what facilities are available elsewhere in your home, you will also have to make decisions about what equipment is needed in addition to the shower or bathtub. For example, it is always useful to have a toilet adjacent to the tub or shower, so that you once undressed you do not have to put your clothes back on to go to another room.

People seeking the luxury of a connecting bathroom are often persuaded to install it in small spaces. While they may be eager to have washing facilities in an integral or adjacent space, they are unwilling to lose valuable floor area in the bedroom. Architectural features such as archways or recesses on either side of a fireplace can lend themselves to being incorporated in a plan of this kind, and extra space may also be found by moving a doorway or incorporating into the bathroom a section of the end of a corridor or passageway.

Ventilation and storage

You might want to conceal a shower or toilet in a built-in closet so it does not encroach on the rest of the room. Ventilation is especially important in such circumstances because of the need to make sure the cabinet or other enclosure does not become damp or humid. If you plan to include a shower in this kind of room, consider a sealed unit, with built-in roof and tray, that will contain much of the steam and water within its walls.

The relative lack of air in a small room means that unpleasant odors tend to linger there longer than they would in a larger room. To counteract this, it is advisable

Above **A wall-mounted sink saves precious inches in a small bathroom. If the sink were built into a unit, it would appear more solid and boxy, making the space around it seem smaller. The curved, wall-mounted towel** rod is also an economical way of heating the room and drying towels without taking up floor area. Right **In a room that is well waterproofed—such as this one, which is completely tiled—a shower door or** curtain may be unnecessary, and an open shower will make the room appear larger. In addition to the overhead shower, there are nozzles plumbed into the wall so water can spray out at various levels.

to install an efficient ventilator and to keep air freshener or a similar perfume-based product close at hand. One option is an electric fan that turns itself on automatically when a light is switched on, or which can be triggered by a device on the door frame that activates the fan when the door is opened.

Although storage space is frequently at a premium in these small rooms, you should ideally avoid putting up too

Brighten a windowless room by placing a small window frame in front of a piece of opaque glass and setting a small light behind the glass to give the impression of daylight beyond.

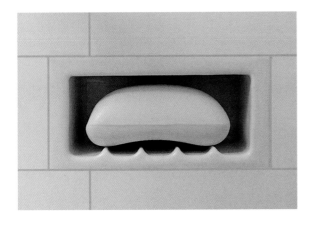

This 1930s' style bathroom has a ceramic tub with a rounded edge, and the walls have been tiled with period-style brick-shaped ceramics. Instead of a rigid shower panel, water-repellent curtains have been hung to complement the rounded shapes of the space. They can be drawn back and decoratively draped when only the tub is being used.

many cabinets or wall-mounted accessories because they will make the walls appear to be closing in and give the impression that the room is even smaller than it is. Keep cabinets and other storage facilities up high, above eye level and preferably above head level, so they are not immediately apparent when you walk into the room. You could build a single narrow shelf around the perimeter of the room so that narrow or smaller objects can be stored there—but, for safety's sake, do not position it over the bathtub, in case things fall off. As long as the items are neatly stored, preferably in opaque watertight plastic boxes, they will not dominate the room.

If you decide to use plastic boxes for storage, make sure they are of a uniform design or colour rather than a jumbled collection, and reserve each box for one type of item—medicines, make-up, or bath potions, for example. Keep the ones you use most frequently close at hand. Those containing less often used items—such as mosquito repellent, or false eyelashes for wearing at parties—can be stored in less accessible places.

Creating an illusion of spaciousness

The decoration of a small room can either add to the feeling of space or detract from it—at worst, the room may be reminiscent of a dark, damp cave.

There are several things you can do to make a small space seem larger. Choosing light colors and plenty of white will brighten up a dark or windowless room. Dark colors can evoke a cozy intimate feeling, but they should be used sparingly—otherwise, the effect may be claustrophobic. If you are passionate about rich dark colors, try using one such color on a single wall and a much paler tone of the same color on the other walls—or use the dark color on the woodwork and the lighter shade on the walls.

Mirrors are a great way of creating an illusion of space, but don't overdo them in a small room—it can be disorientating to be greeted first thing in the morning by a vision of yourself infinitely reflected. If there are no windows in the room, you can introduce a window-style feature by putting a mirror behind a small window frame, or by placing the frame in front of a piece of opaque glass and setting a small light behind it to give the impression of daylight beyond.

Flooring and lighting can also be used to enhance a feeling of spaciousness. For example, if you have a wooden plank floor, you could lay the length of the plank parallel with the longest wall, or toward the door, so that the eye is drawn along the length of the plank. If there is a striped or linear pattern in a linoleum or a vinyl tile, lay it the same way.

If a small bathroom has a central hanging light, the eye is drawn to the level of the illumination, making the ceiling appear lower, whereas a row of recessed spotlights will be neat and flush with the ceiling, giving a more spacious feel.

Useful equipment

Among the fixtures and appliances that have been particularly designed for small bathrooms is the Sitz bath, which has been popular for a long time in Europe. This is a deep square tub with an integral seat. When someone is immersed in a Sitz bath, the water level reaches the height of the upper chest.

There are also many modern bathtubs specifically designed to be suitable for small rooms. They tend to be shorter than the more luxurious styles, and some

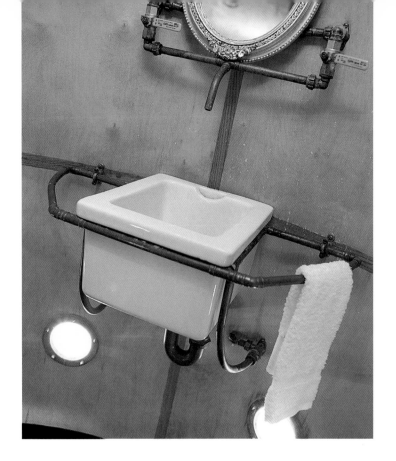

Left **This shower cubicle with circular lights has a pivoting door that closes over to create a watertight enclosure. The inner walls are made of birch-faced plywood, and there are darker strips of veneered plywood where the panels join. The floor is made of slate with a central drain.**

Left **Originally a school laboratory sink, the lav was bought second-hand at an auction. It has been mounted in a copper piping holder and has a single copper spout and institutional-style faucets above.**

of them taper to follow the shape of the body; this means that the head end is wide enough to accommodate the width of shoulders and hips, but the tub then curves inward to follow the line of the legs and feet. Saving space this way may mean you can put a sink at the foot end without having to sacrifice the pleasure of a real bathtub. These tapering tubs are usually available in right- and left-handed versions so they can be used on either side of a room.

If you wash your hair in the bath or shower and feel that a large sink is a waste of space, choose one of the many small ones on the market. These include industrial ones that slot into the wall in an upright fashion, leaving a small recess in the bottom to catch the water. The faucet can be plumbed in at the side of the sink rather than in the center at the back, which also saves space.

There are a number of corner sinks on the market that have been specifically designed to fit into the right angle where two walls meet. These can be useful for installing behind doors or in areas where flat wall space is scarce. The typical sink has a triangular integral ceramic corner that fits between the two walls and the bowl sits in front. This kind of sink can be held up securely on brackets screwed into the walls and does not need a pedestal support.

A towel rod inserted under the front edge of the sink can serve a double purpose. Not only does it provide an appropriate place to hang a hand towel, but also, when the towel is in position, offers a means to conceal the unsightly pipe underneath.

The fact that it is much easier than it used to be to keep pipes hidden is a boon in a small bathroom. Rather than the place being dominated by ugly brackets and long stretches of pipe, most of this functional spaghetti can now be disguised or eliminated. Enclosing the toilet tank behind a half-height false wall, for example, reduces the amount of ceramic on show, and the top of the cover, which should be hinged to give access to the top of the tank, can double as a shelf.

Toilets and sinks that can be mounted on the wall are also worth considering for a small bathroom because the absence of pedestals conveys the appearance of more floor space. If you decide to install such fixtures, allow for a slight overlap, so the edge of the sink can occupy a small part of the area above the toilet bowl—those valuable inches can make all the difference.

Another feature that may need to be introduced into a small bathroom—especially if it the only enclosed space in an open-plan apartment—is a retractable clothesline. A clothesline placed over the tub can be useful for drying lingerie as well as the hand-washed woolens that have a tendency to drip for some time, and it can be wound back into its case when it is not in use.

Showers in small spaces

It is unlikely that you will have space in a small bathroom to accommodate both a shower and a separate tub. If you decide to sacrifice the tub, make up for it by installing a luxurious shower with plenty of bells and whistles, including a multiple showerhead and an adjustable spray. But remember that many people like to have the option of either bathing or showering, and even though your personal preference may be for a shower, think about showing off the apartment to a potential purchaser when you decide to move; offering both a bath and a shower could be a strong selling point, especially if it is your only bathroom.

The usual way to incorporate a shower into a confined space is, of course, to install it over the bathtub, so the tub itself doubles as a shower pan. When it comes to containing the spray from a shower over the bath, the cheapest and simplest option is a shower curtain hung from a pole. The main disadvantage of this arrangement is that a cold plastic shower curtain clinging to your bare skin can be a severe distraction from the pleasures of bathing. Also, although there is an ever wider choice of shower curtains on the market, you may have a problem finding a style of curtain that harmonizes with the existing decorative scheme in your bathroom.

The more satisfactory solution is to erect either a screen made of reinforced glass along part of the side of the bathtub or sliding glass panels that enclose one whole side of the tub. These and other options are examined in more detail on pages 80–91, in the section devoted to showers and wet rooms.

Half-baths

A half-bath is often just big enough to accommodate a toilet and sink; there is generally no room for a bathtub or shower. The bathroom commonly used by guests, a half-bath is also useful, among other things, as a means of dispersing the load on the principal bathroom or bathrooms. In a home constructed on more than one level, a half-bath on a different floor from the main

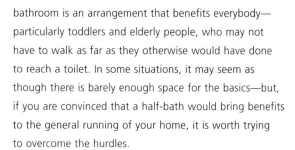

bathroom is an arrangement that benefits everybody—particularly toddlers and elderly people, who may not have to walk as far as they otherwise would have done to reach a toilet. In some situations, it may seem as though there is barely enough space for the basics—but, if you are convinced that a half-bath would bring benefits to the general running of your home, it is worth trying to overcome the hurdles.

There are a number of fixtures on the market that may mean you can transform what appears to be an impossibility into a reality. For example, a leading British manufacturer now produces a toilet seat with a sideways orientation that means you can sit comfortably at an angle, thereby avoiding physical contact with the sink, and perhaps escaping a burn from the radiator.

If your household is predominantly male, a urinal could be the solution—a wall-mounted one would take up less space than an ordinary toilet. There is even news from Scandinavia of the development of a female urinal, but it is not yet in the stores.

Some of the options for sinks in small bathrooms have been discussed earlier in the chapter. It is important in a half-bath, more than anywhere else, to keep the clutter on a sink to a minimum—choose a single bar of soap or a liquid soap dispenser and try to avoid bulky soap dishes and decorative but unnecessary items such as baskets of potpourri.

In a half-bath, as in a small bathroom, it is not advisable to box things in or to install a cabinet under the sink because the resulting structures will take up valuable space. If you really need some form of storage under the sink, a couple of narrow graduated shelves—a wider and longer one at the top, and a narrow, short one at the bottom—will help. The shelves can be concealed behind a canvas or plain fabric curtain that will act as a screen but do no damage if someone sitting on the toilet knocks their knees against it.

Storage units are best installed above the height of the sink—safely out of the reach of children—but make sure you position them carefully so people using the half-bath are not in danger of cracking their heads or poking their eyes on the corners.

The back of the door of a half-bath is a space whose usefulness is often overlooked. The door can be an excellent site for a mirror and towel ring and, if it is within easy reach of the toilet, even a toilet-paper holder.

Below This silver and black paper has a shiny reflective surface, which can brighten up a windowless half-bath. **Below right** Mirror is a useful material behind a sink. **Right** This sink and shower enclosure has a glass wall whose middle section has been frosted—not only enhancing the decorative scheme, but also making it more conspicuous. It is unlikely that anyone would walk into a frosted pane —which might happen if the whole wall were clear glass. The opaque band is at the right height to provide a certain amount of modesty screening for a naked adult.

showers and wet rooms

Showers are exhilarating and refreshing. It is believed in Asia Pacific that the fast-flowing water falling over your body enhances Ch'i, or positive energy. In addition to boosting your vitality, showers cleanse, washing away dead skin and sweat which, if you have a bath, tends to stay in the water with you. In Japan it is common to shower first to cleanse the body, then to sit in a tub of warm water to soak and relax.

Many people find that taking a shower is the best possible way to start an ordinary day—a blast of water from head to foot, washing away sleepiness, relieving stress, and preparing the mind and body for the challenges ahead. There are also situations in which a shower is more appropriate than a bath. For example, a shower after sports or exercise is a marvelous way to cool down and wash away perspiration, and people with mobility difficulties can find it easier to walk into a shower enclosure and sit down than to get up and down in a bathtub.

Showering tends to be a less time-consuming exercise than having a bath. It is also more ecologically sound because it uses considerably less water—a single bath is reckoned to use the same amount of water as several average-length showers.

New trends in showering

A shower has traditionally been installed as an integral part of the bathtub, with the tub doubling as a shower pan, but there is a trend for the two fixtures to be seen as separate items, each of which can offer different benefits. The vogue began as a consequence of the growing popularity of whirlpool baths, when people decided they did not want to close in their stylish new tubs with curtains or doors.

In the search for ever greater luxury, more and more elaborate 'super showers'—characterized by multiple shower heads and finely adjustable sprays—have become widely available, with manufacturers never short of ideas for adding exciting new features. For example, it is now possible to buy super showers with built-in TV monitors and stereo/CD players, in addition to electronically controlled body sprays. Most popular of all are steam units—which are desired for their health-promoting qualities as well as the pleasures they bring.

Technological developments such as pressure-balancing valves, which regulate water temperature and rate of flow, have brought an added degree of safety to the shower. This is particularly advantageous in a household with children. Ideally, it should be possible to turn the water

Left **A roomy enclosure with built-in seating offers the opportunity for some restful contemplation in the warm steam. In spaces where total waterproofing is required, a plastic membrane or liner must be inserted before adding tiles or other coverings.**

Top **Mosaic tiles can be bought in strips on a mesh backing and can be applied easily to large areas.**

Above **Birch-ply veneer provides the interior facing for a shower pod.**

Right **The lining of this distinctive shower enclosure is made of circular ceramic tiles embedded in concrete.**

on and off, and to regulate the temperature, from outside the shower stall. Other important safety features include nonslip flooring throughout the bathroom and at least two grab rails in the shower itself.

Shower seats are becoming an increasingly sought-after element in new bathrooms—either to sit on and perform routine tasks or as a useful surface on which to place bath accessories. Best of all, a seat gives the bather an opportunity to luxuriate unhurriedly in the pleasures of the water or steam.

If you do not want to embark on a complete remodel, there are various ways of adding luxury to your shower without expensive building work. One of these is to replace a single valve with a shower panel that includes multiple shower heads and body sprays.

Choosing showers and shower enclosures

There are numerous styles of shower enclosures to choose from. These include a curtain over the bathtub, a safety-glass panel at the shower end of the tub, shower doors, and a freestanding shower stall or pod.

If you are anxious to economize and/or genuinely prefer having a bath to taking a shower, then you might consider a shower curtain and pole. Curtains are not ideal because they have a tendency to cling to damp skin but, if the bottom of the curtain is tucked well inside the edge of the bathtub, they provide an efficient way of containing the spray from the shower.

Hanging the curtain can be done according to one of two methods. One possibility is to use an L-shaped pole, attached to the wall at one end of the long side of the bathtub and then across the short side. The second, and perhaps more enterprising, option is to use a circular pole hung from the wall that surrounds the area around the shower head. This can look attractive if the shower is positioned over the long side of the tub. Shower curtains are traditionally made of printed nylon or plastic, but in recent years more interesting fabrics and designs have become available.

If the thought of a shower curtain leaves you cold, you could consider a screen made of reinforced safety glass. In its simplest form, such a screen fits along part of the open side of the long side of the bathtub. Although it is not a totally spray-proof option, it is about 75 per cent effective. A more reliable choice is a folding bath screen, which resembles a standard screen but has an extra panel

that slides out beside the fixed one, providing around 16 inches of extra screen to catch the drips. The ultimate over-bath shower enclosure consists of sliding panels that fit along the whole of the open side of the tub. This is ideal if your tub is plumbed in between two walls. If it is not, you may need to buy a single solid panel for the open short end of the tub or build a lightweight, non-load-bearing wall that can be tiled or made waterproof on one side and act as a securing point for the far end of the screen.

Below and opposite page **When planning a shower or wet room, take into consideration the weight of the materials that will be used to cover the walls and floors. In a large space the total weight could be substantial. If the room is on an upper level, beams and joists may be put under a great deal of stress. If slate is** **your preferred option, you may want to find a slim tile for the walls, where they do not have to be so robust, and a thicker one for the floor, where they need to be stronger. Particular care should be taken in grouting between small tiles, especially mosiac tiles, to make sure each and every seam is sealed.**

If your tub is freestanding, another option is to hang the shower curtain or curtains from lightweight movable screens that can be brought out when needed and folded away when the curtain is dry.

Among the alternatives for large bathrooms are a two-sided shower enclosure, a custom-built shower cubicle, and a freestanding shower cubicle. The shower enclosure is a door with one or two side panels; the remaining side or sides of the enclosure are generally the existing wall or walls of the room, which have been waterproofed and tiled or covered in another form of water-resistant finish. The paneled sides are usually made of safety glass—one of them is rigid while the other contains the door.

There is a variety of doors to choose from. The most economical as far as space is concerned is the bi-fold, which is hinged in the middle and can be pulled in toward the person using the shower; sliding doors are also space-saving in that they double back on themselves—but both these options give restricted access. If you have the luxury of plenty of space,

the most satisfactory design is the standard hinged door that opens out and provides a good clear entrance and exit. Another version of this design has, instead of hinges, a vertical column fixed off-center through the door. Pivoting the door on the column opens or closes it.

Some freestanding showers have been designed to dispense with with doors altogether, which makes them a more integral part of the bathroom and cuts down on the surface areas that need cleaning.

The most efficient way to make use of all the space you have available is to create a custom-built shower cubicle. This is similar to the enclosure but does not depend on the pre-existence of two right-angled walls. The custom-built cubicle can be built to fit into any space. It needs a single wall, probably a long back wall; lightweight, non-load-bearing walls, known as stud walls, can be built to create the ends. You will have to decide how large you want the glass doors at the front to be. You can choose a single-pivot or hinged door or a double- or triple-paneled

Above and top right **You may want to create your own shower enclosure to fit the space and location available. Stud and glass walls can be constructed to form a container, and if there is no suitable supporting wall, the shower heads can be plumbed in along the ceiling.**
Right **The floor should be slightly sloping so the water runs naturally toward the drainage outlet.**
Far right **A circular shower pan and curved panel offer ample washing space.**

version, in which the side panel or panels are rigid and the remaining one is the door. Alternatively, you could install a single stationary panel and two doors that open in opposite directions to provide double-width access to the interior of the shower.

This type of cubicle also gives you the flexibility to build the walls up to the ceiling and create an upper section over the door and panels so the shower is totally enclosed. You may also choose to have a multijet shower facility with other shower heads—in addition to the central shower head—plumbed in through the walls at different levels.

As three of the walls of the cubicle will probably be solid, it may be dark inside, although the glass wall at the front will provide some illumination. To overcome this problem, you could install internal lights. The lights,

most often recessed into the ceiling, must be specifically designed for this type of use. Standard fixtures are not routinely sealed and may be a potential source of danger if they come into contact with moisture.

Another idea is to build the walls of the enclosure from glass blocks, which not only let light through but also have good insulation properties. The blocks are available as clear glass or in colors such as green, royal blue, turquoise, and gold—you can use a single color throughout or a mosaic mix of all. Good-quality glass blocks come with a vinyl collar that has interlocking grooves to guarantee the blocks fit tightly on top of each other before they are set with a special adhesive.

The third option is the freestanding cubicle. The cubicle has a shower pan, walls, and roof in one molded pod that can be put virtually anywhere because it does not need to be against a wall. This type of unit is appropriate in a connecting bathroom or where a shower is

needed quickly. It is prefabricated and may be easily installed, and there is no assembly, tiling, grouting, or sealing to be done. Basic units come in a standard design and a choice of pastel colors in addition to white. The modules tend to be practical but not very stylish, with a choice of doors that includes corner-entry, pivot, or bi-fold. Space inside is fairly limited, and some cubicles come with an opaque or clear roof to admit light and relieve the sense of being shut in.

At the other end of the spectrum are spacious freestanding cubicles that come with built-in steam-sauna function, electric lights, and aromatic herb dispenser. They may also have an integrally molded seat and a programmable electronic up-and-down device that allows you to place the water jets where you want them. Some have thermostatic mixers so you can have a shower at your preferred, preset temperature. Foot, back, and vertical massage jets may also be an option.

The pod or freestanding cubicle has an integral shower pan, but in the purpose-built shower cubicle you could seal and tile the floor as well as the walls, creating a miniature wet room. In most cases, however, your preferred option will probably be to build in the largest available precast enameled or acrylic pan. While you are building in the rim on each side of the pan, the area around it can be extended up to create a shelf or, if there is room, a seat.

Shower pans can be found in a variety of shapes and sizes. The standard ones are square, but corner shapes and rectangles are also available, and there are some pans with circular recesses within a square frame. Pans are constructed from various materials including cast iron, steel, composite, and enameled fireclay. More recently, as part of the trend toward more natural and organic materials, stone has been gaining in popularity.

Unpolished stone has the advantage of having its own nonslip surface, but in the case of the enameled and other shiny-surface pans, it is important to have a nonslip finish. Most manufacturers create a raised pattern within the pan, the ridges of which provide a nonslip grip; alternatively you can add a rubber mat, strips of self-adhesive textured banding, or a wooden duckboard.

The problem with many of the textured adhesive strips is that they can, in time, become stained and grubby-looking, and they are difficult to clean. It can be easier to replace them than to try to remove the

Far left **The shower enclosure is an integral part of this bathroom. A large recess has been created by building an enclosing third wall, but the fourth side has been left open to the rest of the room.**
Left **Slim shelves of reinforced glass provide water-resistant storage in**

this rough-textured shower room. The interior walls are constructed from a gray, non-sanded grout that is applied like plaster—a waterproof material more commonly used as a lining for swimming pools. By contrast, the floor of the shower is made of smooth slate.

Right **A large stone- or slate-clad wet room needs heating to insure it is an inviting place to walk into. However, electricity and water are a potentially deadly combination, so any heating or lighting should be installed by a licensed professional.**

Far right, top **This simple disk-backed knob can be easily turned to vary the temperature of the water.**

Far right, bottom **An efficient central drain and cover are essential in a wet room. The cover should have closely set ridges so that small items such as bottle tops and caps are not washed away.**

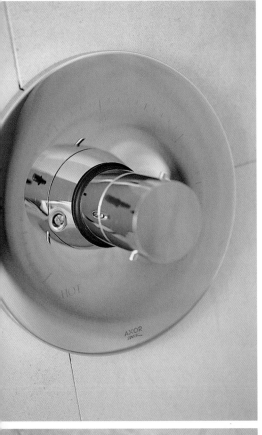

grime. There is no standard height for a shower head. In general, the shower head should be installed at a height that suits you—perhaps 6 inches above the top of your head—but it is worth discussing the options with your plumber. If the shower is intended for family use, it may be preferable to choose an adjustable head that can be moved up and down on a pole mounted on the wall to suit the various heights of different members of the family.

Technological advance has made the experience of taking a shower potentially even quicker and more convenient than it used to be. There are now showers available with temperatures and spray patterns that can be preselected; there are even timers that can make the shower ready for use at the right temperature when the alarm clock wakes you up each morning. The Logic Curva enclosure by Vernon Tutbury has a digital display panel on its exterior that provides an exact temperature readout before you venture in. Comfort is also considered to be a crucial part of the

Many people find a blast of water from head to foot an ideal way to start the day—washing away sleepiness, and preparing the mind and body for challenges ahead.

showering ritual. You may shower at speed in the morning, but at night you may, if space allows, prefer to sit and linger in the moist and steamy atmosphere. To meet this need, manufacturers have produced wooden and stainless-steel shelf-style benches, seats in perforated plastic and steel bucket shapes, and a ceramic ledge that can be tiled onto a sturdy exterior wall.

Although acrylic, fiberglass, and resin mixes are increasingly used in preformed units, glass is still popular for the majority of panels and doors. The type used should be safety glass; for doors and panels this is usually about ¼ inch thick. The glass is offered in plain or opaque panels and sometimes with decorative motifs or patterns in opaque on a clear background or visa versa. You can also buy opaque glass-effect self-adhesive plastic that can be used to create a design that can then be stuck onto the glass. The plastic should be stuck on the dry, outer side of the glass rather than the moist, inner surface so the adhesive properties will not be affected.

Developments in the production and toughening of glass mean that rounded and frameless walls are now possible without being prohibitively expensive. Among other recent innovations is the glass surface that has been treated so water rolls off in beads, taking mineral scale and dirt with it.

Wet rooms

A wet room is simply a shower in a room that has been totally waterproofed. Well established in Europe, the wet room usually consists of a totally tiled enclosed space with a sloping floor and a central drain. It does away with the problems of damp clinging curtains and the restrictions and confines of a cubicle and means more than one person can shower at a time.

Wet rooms should be installed under professional supervision because it may be necessary to line the walls, ceiling, and floor with a polyethylene membrane to prevent leakage. A drain must be sunk into the floor, which needs to slope slightly so the water is channeled into the outflow.

The shower head can be plumbed in through the wall with a simple dial or faucet beneath so there is minimal gadgetry on show. There will also be plenty of space for a small wooden seat or bench and a sauna bucket filled with back brushes and loofahs on hand for a good all-over scrub.

Right and below **Slate has become an increasingly popular finish for the walls and floors of wet rooms and shower rooms. It can be cut in large squares to reduce the number of joints. Slate also has an interesting surface, with grain and texture. Dry slate is a soft shade of gray, and wet it takes on a deeper charcoal color. The dark gray contrasts well with greenish glass, silver accessories, and pristine white towels.**

Opposite page **Two hinged panels of opaque glass mark the boundaries between the different areas of this bathroom. Separated from the rest of the room by a small door, the toilet has its own niche, while a larger glass door swings open to give access to the shower. A horizontal surface of poured concrete provides a useful resting place for towels and other accessories while you are taking a shower.**

Although the wet room is traditionally an open space, you could build in low walls or benches as part of the floor plan. For example, it is possible to incorporate a low ridge around the back of the showering area so a small pool of water builds up and you can stand in it up to ankle height. An alternative is a raised platform about the height of a bench that could be used either to sit on or as a place to put bath products and sponges.

If the wet room is small, it may be sensible to keep towel rods and towels on the wall outside or in a passageway, as stray spray and the buildup of steam may cause the towels to become damp and smelly. If the room is large and the ventilation effective, the moisture should disperse without causing problems. In a wet room where there are a lot of cold tiled surfaces, underfloor or behind-tile wall heating will help take the initial chill off the room. The installation of this type of heating is often done by a professional electrician, but in some places there are systems available for homeowners to hook up to.

The grout between the tiles in a wet room may become stained if the ventilation system is inadequate or if your water contains certain salts or chemicals, so try to find a grout that is mold-retardant as well as recommended for holding its original color. Another potential problem is that the surface of tiles may become dull from constant wetting and drying, and deposits may build up, so they will need regular washing and rinsing. Villeroy & Boch have developed the Ceramic Plus surface, which is so smooth that water, dirt, and calcium deposits run straight off, leaving it clean and shining.

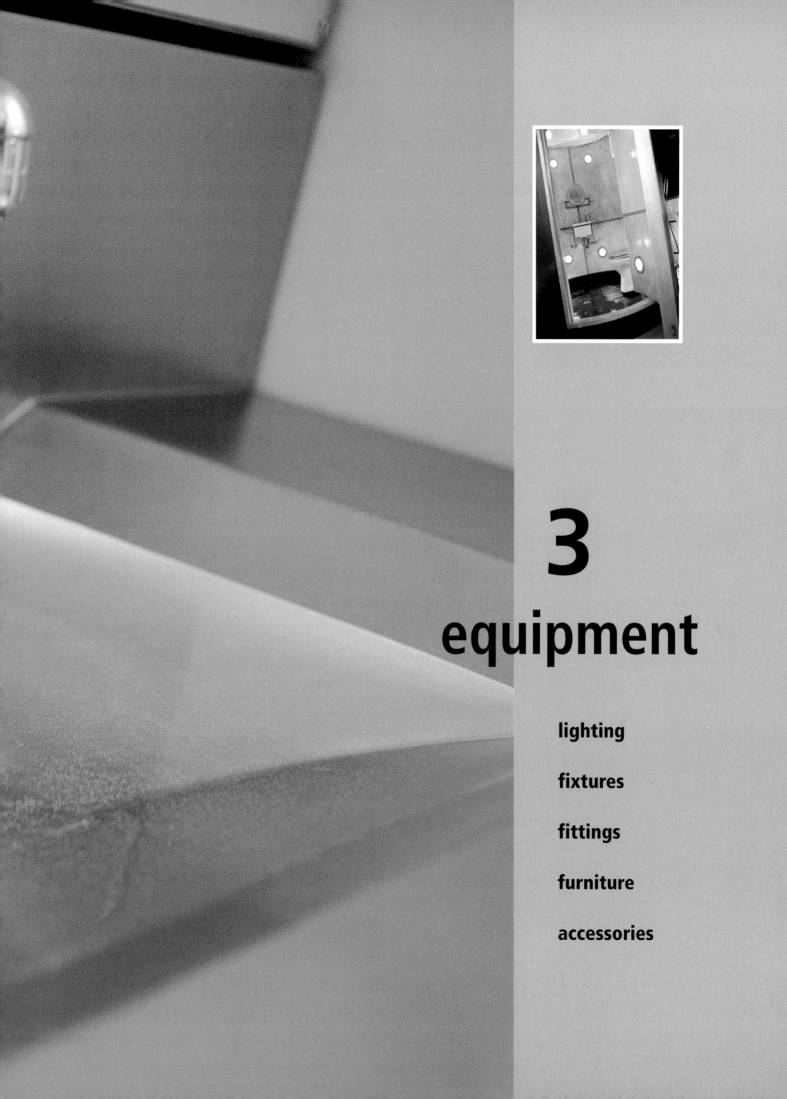

3
equipment

lighting

fixtures

fittings

furniture

accessories

WHEN YOU KNOW WHAT KIND OF BATHROOM YOU WANT AND HAVE SETTLED ON

THE LIKELY LAYOUT OF THE ROOM, YOU CAN START TO MAKE DECISIONS ABOUT

LIGHTING, FIXTURES, FITTINGS, FURNITURE, AND ACCESSORIES. ALTHOUGH

YOUR CHOICES WILL BE RESTRICTED BY THE SPACE AND MONEY AVAILABLE,

THIS IS WHERE COLOR, STYLE, AND MORE FANCIFUL ELEMENTS CAN COME INTO

PLAY—BUT THEY SHOULD NOT BE AT ODDS WITH THE OVERALL AIM OF MAKING

THE BATHROOM A SAFE, EFFICIENT, AND COMFORTABLE PLACE.

There is a bewildering assortment of equipment to choose from, ranging from faucets and shower heads

to tiles and bathmats. If possible, look at the item or finish before buying it, or obtain a sample. Objects

that look glamorous in a pamphlet, professionally lit and expertly styled, can lose some of their shine in

the cold, hard light of a showroom or newly arrived in your freshly plastered bathroom.

The easiest place to start is with the sanitary fixtures because they are the biggest items and usually

come in sets, so the bathtub, toilet, sink, and bidet are in the same or similar shape and have a matching

finish. If you have settled on a definite decorative theme, this will influence your choice of shape and

color. For example, an Art Deco scheme might lead you to choose square, angular designs, whereas a

contemporary plan could direct you to a freestanding glass sink.

Once the set has been selected, and checked to make sure the size and configuration suit your

needs, you can chose the ancillary pieces such as the faucets. Walk around a bathroom or plumbing

showroom and try the various handles until you find one that is comfortable to use and appropriate for

your setting. Plumbing requirements might be dictated by the openings drilled into the rim of the bathtub.

For instance, some tubs have a fixture that has has a single spout with the integral knobs or levers on

both sides. There are other bathtubs that have no faucet openings at all because the faucets and spout

are intended to be wall-mounted—or there may be three separate openings, one for each knob and a

third to accommodate a pop-up drain cover.

Lighting should be carefully planned so that it is functional as well as attractive, and versatile enough

to create a variety of moods and settings. Safety considerations must be very carefully followed when

installing lighting in a bathroom because it is a place where people are often vulnerable and unprotected.

There is not usually much furniture in a bathroom, but a stool can be useful for sitting on to do a

pedicure or manicure. An armchair is a restful spot in which to enjoy the warm, relaxed feeling that

most people experience after a bath or shower. A clothes basket is a practical item that can also be

used as a stool, and a chest or an armoire would be a bonus if you have space for it.

Other accessories will no doubt be influenced by your choice of faucets and fittings. For example,

if you select a chrome or silver-colored finish, then the toothbrush holder, mirror frame, and possibly

the towel rods and other metal-trimmed objects should be of the same finish to give uniformity; this is

particularly important in a small room.

Few safety warnings can be more basic but vital in a bathroom: water and electricity are a dangerous, potentially fatal combination. Any electrical work carried out in the bathroom should be done by a professional. The bathroom is also a place where you are often vulnerable, without clothing that might ground or insulate you from a shock, and your naked skin can be scorched and easily damaged. So, for your own wellbeing, heed all safety warnings relating to electrical fixtures and bathroom lights.

lighting

Any lights or fixtures for use in the bathroom must be specially made for wet places and enclosed in sealed covers or shades to protect them from the effects of steam and condensation. No lighting fixture should be within reach of a person who might be seated or standing in the area of the shower or the bathtub.

Low-voltage lighting can generally be used safely as long as the bulbs are in enclosed fixtures and any sockets are double-insulated. Once the safety factors have been fully comprehended, you can give attention to the creative business of arranging the lighting.

Daylight is the best and cheapest source of illumination. To make the best use of it, you may want to place the sink near the window. Natural light also gives a much more realistic idea of skin tone and color, but no matter how good the natural light in your bathroom is, you will need to enhance it for shaving or other tasks that involve close scrutiny, as well as at darker times of the day or year.

Different types of artificial lighting

A bathroom needs two main types of artificial lighting: the bright and stimulating kind that provides you with a good clear vision of what you are doing, and a low relaxing illumination that is soft and subtle. To achieve the right balance between these two requires good planning. You may also find it useful to have two or more banks of lights and switches that can be operated from a panel outside the bathroom

Above **The opaque window glass allows daylight to penetrate the room but obscures the view from outside.**
Far right **The long narrow panels diffuse the light from outside as it enters the dark shower enclosure.**

Small picture top **A small windowsill can be tiled and used as a shelf.**
Small picture below **Placing a sink beside a window will provide the best access to daylight to assist shaving or the application of make-up.**

and equipped with dimmer switches. Some of these panels can be programmed so that all you have to do is touch the right number for lighting that is bright, mid-level, or specifically targeted. In addition to general and task lighting, mid-level wall lights can be used to soften and even out shadows cast by overhead lights.

To begin with, you should designate a central ceiling area for a functional or ambient light—an all-purpose illumination that you turn on when you enter the room. It can take the form of a central ceiling light or a central row of recessed downlighters. Recessed downlighters

for a separate dressing or make-up table, there is another way to generate regular, well-balanced illumination—by making an arch or border of unshaded pearlized light-bulbs in a style associated with the dressing rooms of Hollywood movie stars. The bare bulbs that form part of such an arrangement may seem basic and unfinished, however, and should be installed only in specially designed safety fixtures.

Task lighting may also be useful where a toilet or shower is in a separate cubicle or recessed behind a wall in an area that has inadequate ambient or natural light. The shower enclosure and toilet can be specifically targeted with downlighters or spotlights.

Other interesting combinations of lighting with an integral secondary feature include a light/ventilator—ideal for a small bathroom because the fan or ventilator is activated as soon as the light switch is turned on. Another variation is the light/heater, which can be very useful in small rooms where one wall is an outside wall and a small radiator is either impractical (due to lack of wall space) or inadequate. A light/heater is mounted on a wall above head height and operated by means of a cord.

Identifying the right fixtures

Even though the selection is limited by safety considerations, there are plenty of bathroom light fixtures to choose from. These range from period-inspired lights with opal glass and chrome finishes to central ceiling lights made up of several adjustable arms that can be arranged to make an interesting shape as well as to give a wide pool of light. Wall lights can be round, oblong, diamond-shaped, or square, and you may find that an opaque finish gives a softer, more diffuse light than clear glass.

A flat disk that screws into a metal plate is not the only type of enclosed shade. There are glass orbs or globes that stand away from the wall on backplates or adjustable brackets. Angular shades that complement the angular lines of Art Deco fixtures can also be found, as can a flamelike glass shade with a fixture that resembles a torch. Bulkhead fixtures, modeled on those used in ships, are both watertight and have nautical overtones that can enhance the utilitarian mood of an industrially inspired chrome bathroom. Although clear or plain glass shades give the most effective light for close scrutiny, colored shades and tinted bulbs can add a decorative or light-hearted element to the bathroom. Lights with colored

Above **A light shining up through a glass shelf illuminates the bottles and vase above, creating a focal point. Some light will also reflect into the small mirror.**
Right **Recessed ceiling lights are ideal for a bathroom, where, for safety, all lights should be enclosed. The light from above has been directed to focus on specific areas such as the wall above the mirror and sink.**

are an appealing idea in a bathroom with a low ceiling because, unlike a ceiling light, they will not intrude upon valuable head room. In addition to functional lighting, you will need task lighting to facilitate shaving, make-up application, flossing teeth, and general body maintenance. This should be targeted on the mirror over the sink, where most activities involving such close scrutiny take place.

Task lighting should offer a clean, even, shadow-free illumination. This is best provided by a strip light with a tungsten or fluorescent tube or by two well-placed and well-balanced side lights. Some mirrors have their own built-in lights, and some fluorescent-strip fixtures have integral shaving sockets. For a mirror above the sink, or

Right Some cabinets and mirrors specifically designed for bathrooms have rows of small lights on each side that cast an even light over the reflection. A combination of lights is used in this bathroom. There are overhead lights recessed into the ceiling, an under-mirror light which illuminates the sink and contents of the shelf, and side lights at the edge of the mirror.

Right, clockwise from top left
Pale shiny walls reflect light, reducing the need for artificial illumination. This small round magnifying mirror has an integral light, making it ideal for close facial scrutiny.
Wall-mounted lights flush to the wall can be decorative as well as useful—the rounded form of the lights complements the shapes of the mirrors and sinks.
These conical opaque shades let light shine through them as well as below.

shades or pale-colored bulbs can be wired on a separate circuit, so the main circuit operates practical lighting while the secondary one operates the mood lighting, which can be used at bathtime or to enhance a relaxing evening shower.

Creating special effects

After an energetic stint in the bathroom with all the lights blazing, you may want to transform the room into a tranquil haven. This can be done by turning off the central light or central section of downlighters and dimming the outer, perimeter lights. Experiment with different combinations until you find the perfect setting for you, the one that makes you feel most relaxed. For example, you could turn out all the lights except for a spotlight trained on the bathtub, or leave the tub in darkness and keep on low lights around the perimeter of the room.

A level of illumination that is restful but not too dramatic can be created by using wall lights controlled by a dimmer switch. Some spa and whirlpool tubs have lights fitted below the water level so that, when they are lit, the inside of the tub and the swirling water become the focal point in a room where the ambient light has been dimmed. Lights that can be recessed into the floor have thick, ribbed-glass, domed lids that screw into a metal casing. Such recessed lights can be used to create pools of light

up walls, in corners, or beside steps leading up to a raised dais area or sunken bathtub, but it is not advisable to install them in the area of the bathroom that is used as a main thoroughfare.

Spotlights—ceiling-mounted or secreted behind a shelf or in an appropriate corner—can be used to highlight particular features. The level of light directed at the feature should be at a more intense level than the ambient light in the rest of the room so the feature stands out.

Candles, especially the scented varieties, have also become a popular source of low-level illumination in the bathroom, but they should be carefully placed so they are not likely to cause a fire. The effect of the soft yellow flames of candles can be enhanced by placing them in front of a mirror or reflective surface. Although candles are romantic when lit, the after-effect of their flickering flames can be less appealing. In the damp atmosphere of the bathroom, the soot emitted from the burning wick can stick to the walls and surfaces, causing a buildup of fine, dark powder. This is easy enough to wipe off tiles or similar shiny surfaces, but it can smear and be difficult to remove effectively from rough plaster and some flat-finish paints. If candles appeal to you, buy smokeless ones.

A touch of decadence especially appropriate for an indulgent bathroom is a chandelier. The play of soft muted light on the glass pendants can create rainbows and starlike bursts. In a room where the ambient light is

low and a pinhole spotlight is directed onto the chandelier, the effect can be very luxurious and romantic, even in an otherwise stark setting. Before installing this kind of fixture, confirm with the supplier that it is suitable for use in a bathroom.

Safety precautions

If you need to change a lightbulb, make sure the area around the light fixture is dry. If you are using a stepladder, check that the floor, especially if it is tiled, is dry and not slippery—you should also have someone else with you to hold the ladder steady. The light should be turned off before the bulb is changed—but, if you have a pull switch, it can be hard to be sure about this because there is rarely a visible indication of whether the light was on or off when the bulb failed. In such a case it is sensible to turn off the main electrical circuit until the bulb has been changed.

Some light shades, such as bulkheads and flush ceiling fixtures, may require a screwdriver to remove the shade. This can be tricky, and you may need a second pair of hands to help you to complete the operation safely: standing on a ladder, using the screwdriver, catching the screws, and holding the shade can be a lot to expect one person to cope with.

If the seal of the shade is effective, the inside should be clean and dust-free. However, if the shade is dirty, take the opportunity to give it a thorough wipe. When replacing the shade, make sure any seal is neatly replaced and that the whole fixture is screwed or clipped tightly shut. Beware of screwing the glass on too tight or it may crack or break.

Above **A sealed, dampproof casing is a vital safety feature in a light fixture.** Right **Recessed floor lighting and glass panels create an interesting combination. When the other lights in the room are dimmed, the effect on the glass is even more striking.**

Top right and far right **Uplights cast dramatic fanlike shafts up an old brick wall. Surrounded by smooth pebbles, which echo their rounded shape, the lights are set beside a floor of wooden decking that reflects the linear arrangement of the bricks.**

fixtures

Solid pieces of bathroom equipment that are usually plumbed into permanent spaces, fixtures include the bathtub, sink, toilet, and bidet, and they come in an ever-increasing choice of shapes, finishes, and colors. Most sinks, toilets, and bidets are made in vitreous china, whose smooth, glass-like finish can withstand high temperatures and strong disinfectant cleaners.

In ancient times bathtubs were made from many different materials, including stone and wood. The Victorians favored heavy cast iron with a glazed enameled finish on the inside of the tub. The acrylic bathtub—a discovery of the 1970s—gave rise to a whole range of new designs because it could be easily molded and colored. It was also lightweight, easy to move, and simple to plumb.

Early acrylic bathtubs were easily scratched and had a tendency to creak and feel unstable because they were relatively flexible; this type of tub is now a much more solid and sturdy part of the bathroom set.

The rise of acrylic-based materials has had a lasting effect on the bathroom. For example, Corian, made by DuPont—a combination of acrylic resin and natural minerals—is used to form shower pans and integral sinks and surfaces. The material is completely solid, non-porous, and will not crack, rot, or warp. It can be cut, carved, routed, sandblasted, inlaid, and thermoformed into a multitude of shapes. Any stains that appear on the surface can be scoured away, and accidental cuts and scratches smoothed with fine sandpaper. The material can also be colored and veined to appear like marble, or incorporated with flecks and fine particles to imitate other stones. It is currently available in around 70 solid colors from the pale to the dark end of the spectrum.

Since the 1990s, other mixes of synthetic and natural materials have been developed, creating hybrid surfaces that are warm and light but strong and durable. Quaryl by Ucosan is made from a fusion of acrylic and quartz stone. The product is fully recyclable, has inbuilt noise reduction properties, and is resistant to knocks and scratches. Like Corian, Quaryl can be cut and molded into numerous shapes and forms. Another composite is Ficore by Design & Form, which is claimed to keep water warm six times longer than standard acrylic.

Traditional and modern bathtubs

Some people love the weight and solidness of a classic cast-iron bathtub, no matter whether it is an original or a reproduction. Genuine old tubs may need some work to restore them to their former glory. The cheapest option is to do it yourself with an enameling kit; this is suitable for covering a small chip or crack, but will be inadequate for correcting

Below **This indulgent bathtub with its paneled surround has been put in the center of the room in front of the window so the bather can admire the view. The tub has double rounded ends and central faucets and hand shower, which means the bather can sit in comfort at either end. The wide rim serves as a shelf, allowing bath accessories to be kept in reach.**

Right and far right **The rolltop bathtub looks as good in a modern setting as in a traditional one. Old cast-iron tubs can still be bought through salvage companies but may need resurfacing. Reproductions are widely available, as are rolltops in lightweight acrylics and synthetic materials.**
Bottom right **If you are putting in an old tub, check that the tub's weight when it is full of water will not over-burden the joists beneath.**

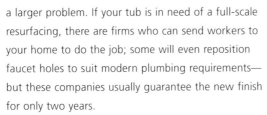

a larger problem. If your tub is in need of a full-scale resurfacing, there are firms who can send workers to your home to do the job; some will even reposition faucet holes to suit modern plumbing requirements—but these companies usually guarantee the new finish for only two years.

For a more permanent and professional finish, the tub can be reconditioned at a workshop or factory. The less expensive option is the infrared lamp system, which reconditions the bath surface. Alternatively, the bath can be re-enameled. This long and involved process starts with the removal of the old enamel by sand blasting, followed by respraying and setting the new enamel in a furnace. The spraying and firing is done about six times so the finish is immaculate and permanent.

The traditional styles, such as the rolltop, can also be made from pressed steel, which is cheaper and much lighter than cast iron and has a more even surface, so the enameling results in a better finish. The process for manufacturing pressed steel is more environmentally sound, and after use the metal can be recycled.

Many modern-style tubs come in other materials, some returning to the inspiration of the ancient Romans and the Japanese, with tubs in stone or wood. Wooden tubs are often made from cypress or teak because those woods have a natural oil that protects the surfaces from the water. Few wooden tubs are entirely watertight, so

This sculptural steel bathtub was custom-made with an undulating base—which allows bathers to sit at the shallow end, to wash their feet, or at the deep end, where they can rest with their legs in a raised position. The design also makes it impossible for the bather to slip down the tub. Bathtubs fashioned from thin sheet metal could cause the water to cool quickly, but most have a double skin that traps air between the two layers, creating a form of insulation and keeping the water warmer longer.

Above **This standing spout arches gracefully over the side of the bathtub rather than interrupting its clean, uncluttered lines.**

Above right and far right **Water therapies and spa** baths are popular, but the plumbing for these machines should be installed so they can be fully drained after each use—otherwise, water may rest in the bends and become stagnant.

Below **A towel rod runs all around the outer edge of this tub. It is not only a practical piece of equipment, but also a decorative feature that breaks up the tub's plain white sides.**

they should ideally be positioned on a tiled floor with built-in drainage. Many also have to be kept filled with water to prevent the wood from drying out and splitting.

The traditional rolltop was a freestanding bathtub with claw feet; its side was left black or painted to match the color of the room. Twenty-first-century versions can be set into a raised plinth to appear sunken, or placed against a wall and enclosed with panels. There are also single- and double-ended options in which both ends are rounded, or one is rounded and the other left square.

Modern manufacturers have emulated the rolltop but given their bathtubs a more contemporary styling. Philippe Starck's design is a freestanding oval bathtub with a thick flat rim and an optional towel rod running just underneath the rim. There are also designs that come with enameled finishes both inside and out, and are raised on an external frame of chrome legs and bars.

Another old-fashioned classic bathtub that can be found in reproduction is the Slipper bath, which has a high raised end, like a hip bath, and a lower rounded end.

Standard bathtubs are generally single- or double-ended and come with an optional apron or side panel used to conceal pipes and plumbing. Alternatively, you can have your own panel constructed from tongue and groove, wood, or whatever suits your room. Usually cheaper than cast iron, acrylic bathtubs have insides that come in a number of different styles: some are plain, while others are slightly sculpted with shaped sides and a slope going down to the base; there are even tubs shaped in a figure-eight that narrows in the center and opens out at each end.

Bathtubs designed to cope with over-bath showers have a wider end to allow more room for movement, and a shower curtain or glass panel. Short and small tubs with tapered sides have been specifically designed for small spaces, and there are also extra-large and extra-deep tubs available. A bigger tub will be heavier and take more water than a smaller one—so, if you are tempted, check that your joists and floorboards are up to supporting the total weight.

Sinks

Sinks come in various sizes and shapes and can be wall-hung, placed on a pedestal, or set into a vanity unit. When deciding on the size and shape of your

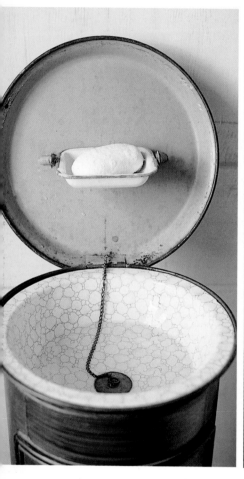

sink, consider how often you use it and what for. If the sink is in a half-bath and used only for washing your hands, it does not have to be particularly large. Deep sinks are necessary only if you require a substantial volume of water.

Many sinks come with a pedestal. This not only disguises the pipes—which are run down behind the recess in the back—but also, if it is floor-standing, provides a place for the bowl to rest. The drawback of a floor-standing pedestal is that it gives you little choice about the height at which the bowl is installed.

Wall-mounted sinks can be plumbed in at a height to suit you, but the piping will need to be led out behind the sink in a special covering. Corner sinks do not often come with pedestals because they are usually set on brackets that are attached to the two

Opposite page, far left **The antique sink in a metal column base with a foldover lid is more for show than regular use. It would be an attractive and unusual talking point in any bathroom.**

Opposite page, left **This sleek streamlined trough is inspired by the sort of sink that doctors and nurses used to scrub up in, and the lever faucets can be turned on and off with the forearm rather than the hands, but it is ideal in a bathroom where a sink is required only for hand and teeth washing.**

Left **Cast-concrete sinks like this one can be constructed to size so that they will fit into narrow or difficult spaces.**

Above **The classic white ceramic sink is still universally popular and works well in most decorative plans.**

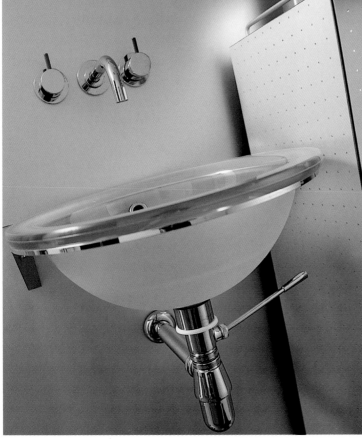

long sides of the sink structure and secured to the walls on both sides. Some sinks are semi-inset into a surround, with the back part slotted into a shelf or cabinet and the front section standing above the surface. The space around the sink is used for a soap dish or bathroom products.

An alternative is the undermount, in which the bowl is set wholly into a surface, often of marble or glass. Some undermounts are edged with a lip or rim that sits on top of the surface. Others have an unglazed rim that sits directly under the opening; the unglazed rim creates a flat, neat seam with the upper surface so there is no gap for water to run through.

A fashionable option for a sink is the bowl and surface mount—apparently a freestanding separate bowl resting on a table or glass shelf. This clean and simple look is reminiscent of the traditional bowl and pitcher used in homes before modern plumbing was invented. The modern bowl has a central drain outlet and the faucet—because it is usually a single sculptural spout and lever—is plumbed to one side, with the spout over the edge of the bowl.

Another modern development is the freestanding sink built into a tall-legged frame that incorporates towel rods, soap and toothbrush holders, a shelf and mirror. This also has a faintly period look that can be traced back to the Victorian washstand combined with a gentleman's valet stand. Another modern design is the Washington sink, which consists of two

Below **Metal sinks need to be carefully maintained. The surface should be finished with lacquer or varnish to prevent tarnish and rust.**

Above far left **This stone sink has a smooth, rounded front and two small, earlike platforms on which to put soap. In contrast with the old and rustic style of the sink, the faucets are modern levers with a single spout.**
Below far left **A glass sink in a steel ring support is ideal for a streamlined or smaller bathroom; its delicate appearance means that it will not seem bulky in a small space. The wall-mounted faucets and spout are positioned at a good height above the bowl so they do not get in the way while you are washing.**
Left **The ceramic bowl on a shelf support is reminiscent of the times before bathrooms were plumbed in, when freestanding bowls were filled with water from a pitcher.**
Right **Square or rectangular sinks are well suited to a bathroom with an angular or geometric scheme.**

concentric stainless-steel spheres. The outer bowl with the drain outlet is stationary, but the inner bowl, which pivots, holds the water while it is being used. When washing is completed, the inner bowl is tipped so the water can run out through the drain in the underbowl.

Glass sinks are another fashionable feature most often seen in architect-designed homes. These sinks look spectacular, but they are expensive and some have to be individually made. Also, being a fashionable concept, they may date quickly.

Toilets

The old-fashioned style of toilet has a raised tank with a bowl at the end of the metal flush pipe. The overhead tank is flushed by means of a chain and handle. Such toilets look appropriate as part of a traditional themed bathroom, but they take up valuable wall space and are difficult to clean thoroughly because there are so many parts.

The close-coupled toilet is probably the most common style, with the tank attached to the bowl by a wide trunk at the back. This is a practical, no-nonsense style of toilet, but it can take a considerable length of time to clean because there are three visible parts: the tank, the joint, and the

Top, above and far right **The finishing touches and details should be in keeping with the overall style and color scheme of the room. For example, these simple understated handles are appropriate partners for unfussy fixtures in a modern streamlined bathroom.**

Right and center top **A ceramic or wooden hand pull suspended from a chain is needed to maintain the integrity of this old-fashioned high-level flush toilet.**

bowl. In the least obtrusive type of toilet—which is uncommon in the USA—the bowl is attached directly to the wall, and the tank is concealed behind a false wall. The tank needs to be a minimum of 30 inches above the floor to provide a satisfactory flush, and the bowl is usually wall-hung, but there are some designs that come with a foot or pedestal.

There are also two alternatives when it comes to flushing the toilet. One is the basic open-rim method, when water is propelled by the strength of the flush along the upside-down, U-shaped rim at the edge of the bowl. The other method is the box rim, where the water is carried in a tube with punched holes in the underside so the water is evenly and thoroughly distributed. The box rim offers the more thorough cleaning system, and is usually quieter.

Increasing awareness of the need to keep water consumption to a minimum has led to the introduction of the maximum 1.6 gallon flush. The reduction from the previous 5 gallon flush rate is a great improvement in terms of saving water, but in some cases has led to a reduction in toilet efficiency. Pressure-assisted toilets can work very well, but some make a lot of noise, so ask for a demonstration before buying. If you are purchasing a new toilet, look for a model with a trap at least 2 inches wide. Seats, handles, and flushing mechanisms should be in harmony with the style of fixture.

Some people like to locate their toilet out of sight—either in a separate room or closed off from the rest of the bathroom by an opaque glass door.

Bidets

A much underrated piece of bathroom equipment, the bidet has been part of the standard bathroom in continental Europe for a long time but has been much slower to become established in the USA The bidet offers benefits in terms of personal hygiene and comfort, and can be particularly useful if your household includes young children, who may need to be washed regularly in the early stages of toilet training.

Bidets also provide relief for people who suffer from medical complaints such as hemorrhoids and for elderly people who find a full bath or shower too difficult as a daily activity. Bidets are either floor-standing or wall-hung; if they are wall-hung, the weight should be supported by a concealed pair of strong brackets.

Top **A Philippe Starck faucet gives the finishing touch to this pair of fixtures—an ultra-modern, wall-hung bidet and toilet. Bidets are available in a wide choice of styles made to match the toilet and the other appliances in the set. There is also a variety of faucets and spouts to choose from. Some people would never be without a bidet, but others cannot see the point of them.**

Left **The classical style of bidet provides an attractive and practical addition to a wide variety of sanitary appliances.**
Above **The old-fashioned slipper design has retained its popularity.**

fittings

Modern fittings are manufactured not only to be attractive and functional, but also to take account of the need to save energy and water. However, safety remains the most important feature of any fitting in a bathroom.

Environmental considerations have led manufacturers to develop faucets that help to conserve water by mixing it with air. The process—described as aerating—reduces the amount of water used without decreasing the power of the water flow.

Sensor technology also helps to save water. Instead of faucets that you turn on manually and may leave running, or faucets that you do not turn off properly, with the result that they drip, the device turns on the water only if it is activated by the movement of a hand under the sensor. Toilets have also been adapted to operate with a smaller volume of water.

At the moment sensor technology is found most frequently in airport restrooms and hotels, but it could become more common in home bathrooms. Until that time, manually operated faucets remain the principal way of getting access to water.

Faucets

Traditional upright faucets were usually found in pairs—one for hot water and the other for cold. In the classic arrangement each one had a knob on top for turning the water on and off, and individual spouts for the water to flow through.

Upright faucets can also be used in a three-hole sink setup in which there are separate hot and cold knobs but no individual spouts; the water is channeled instead through a central spout. An alternative is a mixer faucet, which consists of a central spout with integral hot and cold knobs attached on either side and a lever at the back of the spout that can be raised or lowered to operate the drain outflow.

Bathtub faucets are available in similar styles to sink ones but tend to be bigger. Bidet faucets are usually of the mixer variety with a pop-up drain, and the spout is

Top, far left **Fashioned from copper piping, this faucet was made to accompany a square ceramic sink salvaged from a laboratory.**
Top, center **This long-spout lever faucet with a ceramic cap on the handle would suit a white ceramic sink or rolltop bathtub.**
Above **Most faucets are made of brass and finished in chrome or nickel. A layer of varnish or lacquer is applied to prevent staining and preserve a glossy finish.**

Combining old-fashioned styles with modern technology, faucets and spouts can be made to resemble those used in Victorian times but without the problems of leaking washers. Typical of this design is the ceramic disk faucet, which often gives the manufacturer's name as well as indicators for hot and cold. The style and size of this arrangement suits deep white ceramic sinks with a scalloped backs.

often shorter than those found in a sink; sometimes it includes a directional spray nozzle. The knob or handle of the faucet comes in many forms. Choose a shape that feels comfortable in your hand and a color that complements the rest of the metalwork in your bathroom.

There are no hard and fast rules about pairing old-fashioned faucets with a classic bathtub or modern ones with a modern tub, but in general the simpler the combination of styles, the better the overall effect.

Traditional designs include crossbar faucets, usually available in chrome or brass, and often including raised ceramic disks printed with the words "hot" and "cold."

the crossbar a more contemporary look by the addition of a matte finish such as satin nickel. Satin nickel has a softer appearance than similar, more conventional materials, and gives the impression that the faucet is icy cold with condensation.

Standard fittings such as an upright faucet with a solid knob that is wider at the top and tapers down to the faucet combines elements of classic and modern styles. The knob has indented curves in four sections so it is easier to grip and turn than one with a totally smooth shape. This knob is also available in ceramic finishes that are tinted to coordinate with the color of the tub and sink.

Philippe Starck has designed some curved lever faucets that taper slightly at the top and bottom, which gives them an almost featherlike appearance. In his Starck line, the design is further simplified so that a single lever faucet and a mixer spout with a lever-operated drain form a single sculptural pillar.

Victorian crossbar faucets will tarnish without regular polishing; modern finishes are usually sealed with a varnish or lacquer to prevent this. Although contemporary copies of traditional faucets may have an old-fashioned appearance, they incorporate the latest technology, suchas a quarter-turn facility that makes the faucet more responsive to your touch.

In addition to crossbar faucets, there are ceramic-covered lever faucets that have a similarly old-fashioned appeal. The operating mechanism is opened by pushing the lever from one side to the other. A disadvantage of lever faucets is that it is harder than with normal ones to make sure you have turned them off properly.

As an alternative to traditional chrome and brass finishes, you can give a classically styled faucet such as

The shape of modern spouts has become smoother and more rounded so that they arc over the sink. Some of the levers that operate both the water flow and drain outlet are sleekly slimline, resembling a fine metal rod with small, rounded, buttonlike ends for easier grip. The two most common options for drain covers are the pop-up and the plug and chain. There is also an overflow outlet in case the water is mistakenly left running—if this happens, the water that reaches near the top is siphoned off to prevent overflowing. The overflow is generally a disk to which a plug and chain can be attached. The other choice is a smooth round disk with a concealed semicircular opening at the base; this is usually found in conjunction with a pop-up drain.

Shower controls and heads

Single thermostatic control valves for showers can be operated with either a disk or handle that can be turned from the cold to the hot side of the dial until you find the right temperature. Dual-control thermostatic valves have two functions: one regulates the heat; the other the flow of water. Some of these controls allow you to preset the temperature

Opposite page, far left **The industrial-style, wall-mounted, triangular-headed faucets with S-shaped spouts were chosen to harmonize with the narrow troughlike sink.**

Opposite page, left **A simple lever-action sink faucet supplies mixed hot and cold water through the spout; the lever also regulates the rate of flow.**

Above left **The distinctive Starck three-piece sink faucet with the smooth and sculptural levers has been plumbed in through the sink platform.**

Above **An arc spout rears up in front of the plunge-operated drain outlet. The plunge is depressed to lift the drain cover and raised to close it. The cap of the drain cover is usually a smooth dome that fits neatly into the base of the sink or bathtub.**

that suits the person who will be using it, and the plumbing and pipes can be concealed in the wall. Shower heads are now required by law not to exceed a flow of 2.5 gallons per minute, representing a considerable saving of water over the older ones, which used as much as 6 gallons.

A sliding bar is useful for people who like to be able to change the height of the shower head. The bar is a pole attached to the wall. The head and a flexible hose can be moved up and down it and secured at the desired height by a clip or screw.

Another option worth considering is the needle-spray shower. This is a wraparound tubular shower that resembles an arbor made from piping. The water comes from above and from all of the five circular pipes in the shower, so the water will reach you no matter what height you are.

Shower heads are also available in a variety of sizes and shapes. The disk diameters of the traditional shower head range from 5 to 12 inches.

Left **The upper, stationary shower head supplies a broad spray of water at a constant level, while the lower one can be adjusted so the flow of water varies from heavy massage strength to a light sprinkle. In some cases, it may be necessary to install a pump to create enough pressure for a good flow of water.**
Opposite page, clockwise from top center
A modern flexible shower head with fine spray.
A traditional-style concealed shower control.
A thermostatic temperature control— the hot and cold water are supplied from separate inlets but exit through one outlet; the smaller knob is the
open-and-close device used to operate the waste outlet.
A traditional rigid shower head. Detail of a shower head on a flexible hose.
A traditional crosshead faucet. This bath/shower mixer with lever is a classic fixture in which the shower head sits in a cradle above the faucet.
A four-faucet bath/shower mixer with a single metal spout—two of the faucets supply water for the bathtub; the other two supply the shower head above.
Center **A modern, dual-control thermostatic valve: one knob regulates the flow of water, the other the water temperature.**

so you can simply walk into the shower and turn it on—there is no need for guessing and manipulating until you get it right. A dual-control panel is similar to a single one, but has two knobs or levers, or sometimes inner and outer disks.

Pressure-balancing valves, which are now more common than thermostatic valves, keep the water temperature constant when water pressure changes. For example, if you are in the shower and someone elsewhere in the apartment flushes a toilet, the pressure-balancing valve keeps the temperature constant.

Shower heads are either stationary or flexible. A stationary head that comes with its own integral arm can be installed directly through the wall or attached to a separate shower arm. It can be plumbed in at a height

There are also many adjustable shower heads on the market that offer a choice of sprays. The water in this type of head is often aerated, which gives it a bubblier quality—although such a system reduces the amount of water required, it does not compromise water pressure. You can gently manipulate the head of a variable shower until it reaches the desired type of spray; the range includes full-force spray, intermediate, and concentrated needle spray.

One final option is a traditional-style flexible hose and shower head attached to the faucet that can be plumbed into the side or at end of the bathtub, or on a single, rigid pipe standing beside it. This type of shower is adequate for a quick rinse or for washing your hair, but it is not ideal for regular daily showering.

Ventilation

When the business of showering or bathing has been completed, the condensation and steam that has been generated should be expelled from the bathroom as swiftly and efficiently as possible. A buildup can lead to damp surfaces and the possible growth of mold or fungus. It may also give rise to unpleasant damp smells, and cause damage to wooden furniture, paneling, and accessories.

It is generally not enough simply to open the window. You will have to install an exhaust fan, but how large and powerful a fan you need depends on the size of your room. The cheapest method of mechanical ventilation is a simple plastic fan that can be set into the top of the bathroom window. This can be activated by pulling an on/off cord.

If you are buying a fan for bathroom use, choose an exhaust rather than a recirculator model. The purpose of the fan is to disperse any moisture and unpleasant smells—not to recycle them around the room. An exhaust system extracts the air—that is, removes it from the room.

The level of noise generated by the fan is particularly important if your bedroom is next door to the bathroom—the whirring and the sound of the motor could keep you awake for half an hour after a nighttime visit to the bathroom—so ask for a demonstration of the fan in the showroom before buying it.

Heating

As an alternative to the more traditional forced-air systems, underfloor heating has much to recommend it in a bathroom—providing ambient heat without taking up precious space. It makes possible the use of hard-flooring materials such as slate and concrete that were previously thought too cold for use in the bathroom. Underfloor heating is especially effective when used in conjunction with heated towel rods.

In addition to thermostatically controlled heating elements that run under the floor, there are systems such as trench radiators that slot in level with the floor in a band at the wall's edge. There are heaters that can be recessed into the floor or wall-mounted, and panel radiators that are thin, plain, and unobtrusive and can be recessed into a wall so the finished effect resembles that of an architectural panel.

A panel radiator can be adapted for use as a towel rod by clipping rails or pegs over its frame. Buy ones that are specifically designed to work on your radiator; ordinary plastic hooks may melt and adhere to the panel.

Serpentine curved radiators introduce a sculptural dimension to a bathroom. The Hot Spring radiator, inspired by a three-ring-binder notebook, was designed by Paul Priestman and provides a vertical, pillarlike source of heat that is a feature in its own right. Other coiled radiators finish at the top in a ball finial that can be used to hang a bathrobe.

Wall-mounted horizontal pipes—which are generally evenly spaced or staggered in groups of four bars—can add to the visual interest in a bathroom as well as providing an efficient source of heat. Standard copper pipe that has been bent into a large double curve can also be an unusual but practical feature on a bathroom wall.

Whatever your heat source, make sure it is in an area where you are unlikely to touch it accidentally with your bare skin.

Above and below A heated towel rod mounted on the wall is an invaluable bathroom accessory. Towel rods occupy a minimal amount of space and perform a dual function: they provide heating for the room and offer a means of drying damp towels and other items. The rungs of the ladder-style heaters shown here are often spaced in groups to make it more straightforward to hang things up to dry and also to give the heaters a more interesting, attractive appearance. This type of radiator is available in a wide variety of colors, ranging from the traditional silver/chrome to white and black, as well as a rainbow assortment of colored enamel finishes.

Opposite page, far left A plunger waste control has been teamed here with an equally old-fashioned crosshead chrome faucet.
Opposite page, top Concealed valves are a feature of these streamlined lever faucets and spout that have been mounted onto the wall.

Opposite page, middle These stylized faucets and spout with a retractable, flexible shower do not occupy much space, even though they are mounted onto the platform surrounding the bathtub.
Opposite page, foot The wall-mounted spout in chrome with rounded faucets is a popular design.

Heated towel rods

Specially designed heated towel rods are not generally powerful enough in themselves to provide adequate heat in a bathroom, but they have the effect of topping up the ambient heat supplied by underfloor or central heating. They are also useful for drying and warming towels and other items.

Most heated towel rods obtain their power from a central-heating or hot-water system, although there are some that can be heated electrically—but these tend to be less efficient.

The most popular type of heated towel rod is a traditional ladder-style rail finished in chrome, nickel, or gold effect. The ladder towel rod is commonly available in the form of a simple freestanding design or as a wall-mounted version.

Another option, based on the ladder style, is a double-sided rod with an arched top and two sides of rails, back and front. The double rod gives more space for spreading towels out and for the air to circulate around them and promote drying. An alternative to the arch top is the square top, which allows the towels to be fanned out

over the lower rods. Simple modern heated rods follow the ladder-style design, but whereas the conspicuous joints are a feature of the old style, the contemporary version is a smooth, seamless shape. A simple angular S-shaped rod that provides three horizontal bars for towels is also available.

A narrow three-bar vertical heated towel rod can be used in small spaces. This type of fixture is ideal in a gap between the sink and toilet—a space too tight for a conventional horizontal radiator. What this style of heater lacks in width it makes up for in height, and the overall area emitting heat is comparable to that of the horizontal version.

The concept of the designer towel rod has grown out of the development of the radiator. Although they are undeniably functional appliances, towel rods are now designed in a range of interesting shapes, from crossover X styles to bow-fronted arcs. They are also available in a choice of different colors. No longer confined to the space under the window, they can be found standing pillarlike up the full height of a wall or as a brightly colored panel in an otherwise plainly decorated room.

Far left **This Cobra-therm radiator offers several cross bars on which towels can be hung to dry. It is available in several sizes.**

Above left **A cobra radiator on a swing mount allows the air to circulate around it freely, not only to warm the air in the room, but also to encourage the evaporation of moisture from damp towels.**

Above **A panel radiator has been set into a recess and a towel rod positioned above it so that anything hanging from the rod benefits from the heat. Placing the radiator in the recess reduces the likelihood of its causing burns by coming into contact with bare skin.**

furniture

Styles in bathroom furniture have changed radically from the days of built-in cabinets that mimicked those in the kitchen—where the look had also become very rigid. There is now a strong preference for freestanding simplicity with minimal clutter.

In the 1970s and 1980s, the vogue for creating built-in cabinets in melamine with undermounted sinks and for paneling the sides of the bathtub gave bathrooms a somewhat monotonous sameness. Materials, including laminates and paneled doors, also came to resemble those used in the kitchen, but lighter, pastel shades were favored in the bathroom, and faux marble was preferred to simulated pine.

The trend is now toward a more open feel. Of the few items of furniture found in the bathroom, most are made of real wood and marble or composites of acrylic with marble or stone powder. Where before there might have been a wall of cabinets there may now be only one or two; these are often well constructed from a natural material and finished with plain paint or lacquer that almost merges with the wall color so that they become invisible.

Tall storage cabinets, reaching from the ceiling to the floor, can be disguised behind panels without any obvious opening device—the doors appear to be part of the wall. Putting gentle pressure on a door activates a spring mechanism that opens the door to reveal the shelves or hanging space inside.

The interest in simplicity and minimalism can be seen in the work of a number of designers—for example, the understated square wooden table that supports the Philippe Stark washing bowl, and the fine pillarlike columns found in Dieter Sieger's Bagnella line. The trend is also clear in the rise of the wall-hung sink, bidet, and toilet and the decline of the boxy units and traditional pedestal supports that were once the main forms of support for sinks.

Some modern bathroom fixtures are actually designed to look like pieces of furniture. For example, there is a piece called a console sink, which has two shapely turned

Opposite page, top far left **The classical appearance of these raised-panel cabinets complements the reception-room style of decoration. The black marble surround and splashback, the bust and glass vase, framed paintings and gilt-framed mirror give the room a formal feel.**

Opposite page, top left **Round knobs are preferable to angular ones at lower levels of the bathroom, where you might bump into them and bruise or hurt yourself.**

Opposite page, bottom **Tall paneled doors conceal ample shelf space where linens can be stored, but in a room where steam and moisture are a daily presence there must be good ventilation to prevent the linens themselves from becoming damp.**

Left and below left **The furniture in this room— a double-door cupboard and a cabinet in a similar style under the sink—have been painted white, the** same color as the walls, so they blend into the background of this small bathroom, rather than assuming a dominant role.

Below **This bathroom/ dressing room incorporates shelves for towels and sheets, and hanging space for clothes, as well as drawers and cupboards under the basin and vanity unit. Dressing is given more prominence than washing in the decor of this compact but well-designed room.**

legs like a conventional console table that you might find in a foyer, but the legs are ceramic, as are its top and undermounted sink.

Where built-in furniture is found in the contemporary bathroom, it tends to be in the classic style, based on Biedermeier or even Mackintosh. It is frequently made from a wood that has either been stained or left natural, but varnished or sealed. Glossy laminates have also been replaced.

Where formerly there might have been a laminated area around a sink, it is now more usual to find that the bowl has been designed as an integral part of the surround and raised backsplash, and that all the elements are fashioned from the same material. This may be steel, perhaps, or one of the resin composites such as Corian or Quaryl.

The ability to mold these continuous single pieces means that there are no seams, cracks, or crevices for water to trickle down, and that the surfaces can be wiped clean much more easily. The silhouette of the furniture that supports this type of sink has, as a result, also become more streamlined.

Another feature of the modern bathroom is incorporated furniture. This differs from the built-in variety in that it is sculpted as an integral part of the wall or setting rather than conceived as a unit built up against the wall.

Incorporated furniture embraces such items as a curved seat built out on a base from the wall and butting up against the side of the shower. It could also include one or two steps set against the wall in a wet room—these may be tiled or covered in plaster with a waterproof finish that matches the finish of the main

wall or floor, but they are regarded as part of the structure of the room rather than as pieces of prefabricated furniture.

Old pieces in new settings

There has also been a long-standing tradition of undermounting sinks into existing pieces of furniture such as a Victorian marble-topped kitchen cabinet or an Arts and Crafts chest— even architects' map chests have been used. This type of unit is often used in a bathroom that has an indulgent decorative theme, and if the furniture is in a particularly attractive style or color of wood, it may be echoed in a wooden toilet seat or a chair.

Glass-fronted chests of drawers once seen in notions departments are among the old pieces of furniture that have found a place in the modern bathroom. The glass panel at the front of the cabinet means that its contents can be clearly seen, and its tall, slender shape is timeless and unobtrusive but offers plenty of storage space. Old armoires are also found, sometimes stripped of paint and left in their natural wood color, or pickled or washed to give them a pale, clean finish.

Many of these classic pieces of furniture appear less chunky and heavy than built-ins because they have legs, which means that you can see underneath them. Built-in units usually have a plinth base to cover their adjustable metal legs. Filling in the gap between the base of the cabinet and the floor gives the piece a more solid and fixed appearance, whereas light passes beneath an old-fashioned cabinet and makes it seem less permanent. Shaker-style bathrooms are characterized by simple but

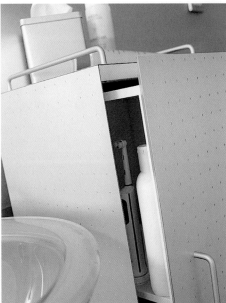

Opposite page **The attractive shape of this conical unit makes it a feature in the overall decorative scheme. The cabinet doors require no knobs or handles because a magnetic spring catch inside each of them can be released by gently pushing on the door itself. Closing a door is equally simple—you simply bring it back into contact with the magnetic catch, which will hold it until it is released again.**

Top right **The plainer and more streamlined the cabinet doors in a bathroom, the fewer niches and crannies there are to collect dust.**
Center right **Convenient D-handles are used to slide open the shelves of this capacious cabinet.**
Bottom right **Storage space in this bathroom consists of a carefully thought-out combination of drawers and open shelves.**

well-crafted wooden furniture. In this case, the style is traditional, but the manufacture is modern. Many companies will build Shaker-style units to order so they can be tailor-made to fit around awkward plumbing or in spaces that cannot accommodate a standard-sized unit.

The simple paneled doors and uncomplicated lines of the Shaker style can help to create the impression of an efficient no-nonsense bathroom, but the mellow color of the natural wood or a soft wash of traditional Shaker shades of blue or red gives a more indulgent and homey feel than other starker and more streamlined designs.

Cabinets

Storage is especially important in the streamlined or Zen-style bathroom because the minimalist look requires the room to be free of clutter. There are also safety reasons for avoiding clutter in that it reduces the danger of tripping and sliding or slipping on objects left on the floor or at the edge of a surface. Instead of a couple of small cabinets, you may find that one large one will do the job and take up less floor space because

Far left **Bathroom cabinets and storage units should ideally have smooth and rounded handles, which are less likely than angular ones to cause bruising if someone bumps against them.**

Center **This dresser has a wavelike sculptural quality that enhances the comfortable and soothing character of the bathroom.**

Above left **If a bathroom is also used as a dressing or laundry room, clothes and bed linen may be stored there, but you should make sure that any buildup of steam and condensation can be swiftly and effectively dispersed; if ventilation is poor, the fabrics may become damp and moldy.**

Below left **By subdividing drawers into smaller spaces, you can increase the number of items they hold.**

the storage area is confined to one tall, narrow unit rather than two or more small and wide ones. The most common place to put a cabinet is under the sink, but the new styles and designs of sinks—which may incorporate column supports and delicate table-like structures—could mean that storage space will have to be found elsewhere.

The storage of medicines should be carefully planned to make sure they are kept under lock and key, well out of the reach of children. Even a medicine cabinet high up on a wall will not deter a curious child from climbing up onto a stool to have a look inside. Bleach and any other toxic detergents should also be stored in a secure place.

Seats and day beds

If you need to sit down in a bathroom, it is much more comfortable to have the option of using a seat than to try to balance on the thin hard rim of the bathtub. The most suitable type of chair or stool depends on the size and style of room. A simple but sturdy stool can also be helpful for small children to stand on so they can wash their hands at an

adult-height sink, and to allow toddlers to reach the toilet with ease—but such a stool must be of the sturdy four-legged variety, and it should be used only under adult supervision.

In a wet room, steam room, or good-sized shower room, a simple slatted wooden stool can be a bonus. In the steam room you can either sit on the stool or, if the room is large enough, lie down and use the stool to raise your feet above shoulder level—which is both relaxing and said to be beneficial to blood circulation. In a shower or wet room, the stool can also be used as a table for setting down soap, shampoo, or loofah or as somewhere to sit when washing your feet.

In a good-sized bathroom, a chair can be used to put clothes or towels on while you are luxuriating in the bath, or to sit on while you are applying nail polish or carrying out a pedicure. As the chair may be the only freestanding piece of furniture in the room, and therefore a point of interest, it should be attractively designed and well finished, as well as in harmony with the rest of the decoration.

If the bathroom is large enough, a day bed or chaise longue is an indulgent accessory. In a streamlined or minimalist room, this type of furniture is acceptable if the structure itself is very simple—perhaps a wooden bench with a futon or thin cushion on top or a stone slab, like a Hammam massage block, with a padded terrycloth cover. There are also a number of classic design pieces that would be appropriate in a simple uncluttered setting. Examples include Jasper Morrison's Three sofa, which

Opposite page **Built-in units provide useful storage in a small bathroom. Here the mirrored cabinet has been fitted into a recess above the sink with a shelf beneath.** Left **Deep, narrow shelves slotted into in an otherwise wasted space can have all sorts of uses in a bathroom that is also used for dressing.** Right **Some freestanding items, such as this sink set into a tablelike structure, bear a close resemblance to traditional furniture.**

has straight ends, but the interior curls and undulates, almost like a body shape, to form two seats. The bent laminated wood and webbing of Alvar Aalto's Model 43 would also be suitable in a bathroom setting because the shape is clean and simple, and the webbing structure will dry easily if it becomes damp. Marcel Breuer's aluminum slatted reclining chair No. 313 with beech armrests is ideal because it has no fabric or upholstery that is vulnerable to water damage.

A day bed in an indulgent style of bathroom could be a classic Victorian chaise longue, an old dentist's or barber's chair with leather upholstery and chrome hardware or the classic Le Corbusier recliner. However, you need to be cautious about using upholstered furniture in a bathroom because the humidity may affect not only the fabric covering of the chair or bed but also the stuffing or padding in the seat and back. Try to position any upholstered furniture as far away from the bathtub or shower as possible and make sure the room is thoroughly ventilated after every use.

Furniture specially designed to withstand damp or wet conditions, such as patio or beach furniture, may be useful in a bathroom. Plastic outdoor seats and recliners are not usually particularly attractive and can be very sweaty to sit on, but the classic wood and canvas director's chair is an option—it has the advantage of being lightweight and foldable so that it can be stored out of the way when not needed, and the canvas dries quickly if it becomes damp.

The classic liner chair with footrest made its way to dry land from the ocean-going ships of the 1930s and 1940s. The modern versions are equally stylish and should be made of treated or well-varnished wood that can cope with the temperatures and

Above **A wicker and wood chair with simple arms looks inviting, but may need to be draped with a towel before you sit on it—otherwise, the pattern from the seat will be imprinted on your skin. Freestanding furniture can add to the comfort and relaxation of the bathing and showering ritual.**
Right **Rather than balancing on one foot or perching on the cold narrow rim of a tub, it is easier to perform a pedicure or manicure when sitting in a suitable chair. Doing your hair or applying make-up is also easier and more comfortable when you have the benefit of a dresser.**

Opposite page, top **In stream-lined bathrooms and shower rooms, a stool or table tray may suffice. You can put all the lotions, oils, soaps, and other accessories you might want on the tray and take it where it is needed. If you choose a wooden tray, make sure it has a water-resistant finish so it will not warp as a result of frequent exposure to water.**
Opposite page, bottom **This simple slat stool can serve as a table as well as being used as a seat in a shower or sauna.**

cabinet with a mirror for applying make-up or for checking that your tie or collar is straight. Such a piece of furniture has the bonus of providing additional storage space, allowing you to put some of the objects that might have rested on the side of the sink on the top of the dresser or in its upper drawers.

This area will also be useful for keeping jewelry that can sometimes accumulate around a sink. Watches, rings, and earrings are common culprits. If the surface of the dresser is wood, use glass or ceramic dishes to protect the finish from the damp bases of bottles and the acid effects of perfumes and aftershave lotions.

Trolleys

Trolleys are mobile shelves on wheels. Many of the units illustrated in fashionable magazines and interiors supplements come from medical establishments such as hospitals and dentists' offices. The simple chrome legs, resting on castors or rubber-trimmed wheels, support glass or metal shelves, that are lightweight and easy to wipe clean.

Trolleys make it simple to move shampoos, bath products, towels and sponges from beside the bathtub to the shower enclosure or the sink as and when they are needed. This means that you only have to have one set of bath products rather than three separate sets—one for each area of the room in which you might choose to wash.

conditions of a bathroom. A liner seat is usually made of wood, so you may need to put some padding over the frame to make it more comfortable—a cushion of this sort should be removable so that it can be taken outdoors to dry.

Dressers

If you have a connecting bathroom or one that doubles as a dressing room, the items of furniture that you choose for the bathroom should be sympathetic in style and finish to those used in the linking or adjacent rooms, to create a feeling of unity and purpose. In a dressing room or bathroom, you may want to have a traditional dresser or

Above and above right **A mirror is an essential piece of bathroom kit. This one has been placed on the front of a recessed cabinet. The mirror appears to have been hung directly onto the wall, but it is in fact concealing useful storage space.**

Right **Wherever possible, store cotton balls, facial tissues, and other cosmetic items that are left on show in covers or holders that resemble each other.**

Far right **If you have space, bottles of oil or bubblebath can make an attractive display.**

accessories

In the streamlined bathroom, accessories should be kept to a minimum. Only items used on a daily basis should be allowed to stay on open shelves and surfaces. In the indulgent bathroom, a few more objects may be put on show, but not so many that the room looks cluttered and messy. There are some accessories that no bathroom should be without—including a mirror and a toilet seat.

Oils and other bath preparations can be left on show in the bathroom, but for display it is a good idea to decant them into matching bottles or containers that have a similar appearance. The containers can also coordinate with jars or boxes in which you keep dry cosmetic aids such as cotton balls for removing make-up.

Joss sticks and incense cones scent the air and add a certain mystical smokiness. You can buy joss-stick holders or trays that have small upright pillars into which the sticks can be slotted. Otherwise, you can create your own with a bowl and some sand. The joss sticks will stand upright in the sand in the center of the bowl, and the ash will fall safely on the sand by the rim.

Many of the beautiful handmade soaps on the market are made with natural organic products such as oatmeal or herbs, which are sometimes suspended within a translucent bar. A few bars can be arranged in a bowl or glass jar and set on a sill by a window to make an attractive decorative feature.

Other washtime accessories include loofahs, real sponges, pumice stones, and brushes to stimulate circulation and remove dead skin. These natural products not only do their jobs extremely well, but they also look attractive and can be arranged to dry on a decorative dish or bowl. Synthetic sponges tend to become slippery and smelly after a short time —something that will never happen to a natural sponge if it is left to dry thoroughly in an open space.

Loofahs make good back brushes, and their rough texture has a slightly abrasive effect on the skin that can be useful for removing dead cells, leaving the skin fresh and revived. Pumice stone can help to reduce areas of hard skin that build up on the heels and soles of the feet

and the elbows. Oriental soaping brushes are useful for stirring up a soft sudsy lather in which to wash your face and body. The suds can be applied to the body in a circular motion to stimulate blood circulation.

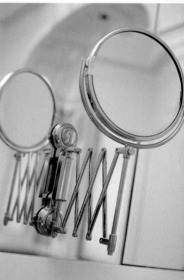

Mirrors

Mirrors are an essential part of a bathroom, not only because they allow you to see yourself during the rituals of teeth-brushing, shaving, and applying make-up, but also because they reflect light and make the room seem more airy and spacious than it is.

Among the most useful are non-mist mirrors, which do not steam up when the rest of the bathroom does. You can choose between those with a specially treated surface and those that are backed with a wafer-thin heating pad. The heated mirror has a minimal surface temperature, and running costs are very low.

A bathroom may need two types of mirror: an ordinary one for general maintenance and a magnifying one for activities that involve close scrutiny. There are large normal mirrors that have a magnifying inset, and others in which a magnifying mirror is attached on an adjustable arm to the rim of a larger mirror. Some mirrors double as cabinet doors, and many are framed by the outer rim of the bathroom door. Mirror panels on sliding doors are also

Top right Small magnifying mirrors are invaluable for close scrutiny. Some, such as the one shown here, are on a rigid wall mounts, but can be adjusted to achieve a better view.
Center right **This model has an extending arm with a magnifying mirror on one side and a normal mirror on the other.**
Bottom right **Another option is an extending mirror on a bi-fold arm—a model that is particularly easy to manipulate.**

available, and some cabinets have integral overhead lights so that the mirror is directly illuminated. A round or oval mirror makes an interesting alternative to the more traditional square mirror. A round mirror can be used to imitate a porthole in a bathroom with a nautical or submarine theme. Long vertical mirrors, usually found in the bedroom, can be desirable if the bathroom is also the place where you do exercises.

Shelves and racks

If you have plenty of wall space in the bathroom, try to place soap trays and shelves in close proximity to where they are needed. For example, an open-mesh wire-rimmed shelf is a practical accessory to have in a shower enclosure: the water can run through the open construction rather than leaving bars of soap melting in a puddle; the rim will stop things from sliding off and ending up around your feet; and the shelf will hold shower gel, shampoo, conditioner, and everything else you need in the appropriate place.

Open-mesh, wire-cornered shelves are also available, including sets of small shelves arranged in a vertical fashion that may be useful when installed above a bathtub. Recessed ceramic shelves may have an attractive appearance, but it can be difficult to reach objects set at

Opposite page, far left **A simple old wooden box can provide useful storage for dry items such as spare bars of soap, cotton balls, and facial tissues.**
Opposite page, left **Soap can also be stored with linens,** such as towels and sheets; its perfume will permeate and freshen the linens.
Opposite page, below left **Bathroom scales are an indispensable accessory for those who like to keep track of their weight. A wicker** hamper is a convenient place to store spare towels or toilet paper.
Below **Old jars from grocery stores, pharmacies, or candy counters can make attractive containers for bathroom products.**

the back of them, and they can become slimy and grubby with residue from soap and other lotions which accumulates and, when it is dried on, becomes hard to remove.

An old-fashioned accessory that survives because it does its job well is the classic bath rack. Open-mesh metal types allow water to drip off sponges, washcloths, and soap and back into the bathtub. The classic bath rack is a purely functional accessory, but some versions have been modified to include a central section that tips up to support books, magazines, and candle holders.

Glass shelves are often installed in front of the mirror and above the sink. They should be made of reinforced glass, either clear or opaque, and supported either by simple caps that slide over the ends of the glass or with metal rods that clip around the glass and hold it firm. The glass is likely to become marked with drips from bottles or tubes and will need regular cleaning.

A cup attached to the wall and a soap dish either resting on the sink or attached to the wall help to keep some of the clutter off shelves. The cup may be a glass, plastic, or ceramic and can be held in a metal or plastic ring. The soap holder should be in a coordinated style. If you use liquid soap, you may be able to do without a soap tray. For solid soap, try to find a dish with a removable perforated tray that allows the excess water to drip away and lets the soap dry more quickly and efficiently. The water that collects in the tray can then be easily thrown away.

Laundry baskets

A bathroom is the place where people commonly divest themselves of their dirty clothes, and a laundry basket is often found there. In addition to its functional role, however, the basket or container for laundry can be an interesting decorative feature. Before buying such an accessory, decide how big you need it to be based on the volume of laundry that your household generates. If you take bed linen and bath towels directly to the washing machine, the basket in the bathroom need hold only small items. Also, if you use a dry cleaner or shirt-laundering service for large items of clothing, it will be needed simply for underwear and lightweight items such as T-shirts.

Laundry baskets come in many shapes and sizes. Choose one with a lid—to keep soiled clothes from view and also, especially if you do your laundry only once or twice a week, to contain any odors that may be emitted.

This page **Items frequently left out on the edge of the sink include soap and toothbrushes. Specifically designed toothbrush racks can be attached to the wall, but many people favor the tooth glass or a cup that rests beside the sink and can be easily washed out when it becomes soiled.**

Toilet seats and roll-holders

Most common designs of of toilet seat are made from molded plastic in a range of plain colors from which you can choose one that matches or complements the color scheme of your room.

Victorian-style bathrooms usually have wooden toilet seats, but these can also be found in modern bathrooms. Wood not only looks more attractive than plastic, but also has the advantage of feeling warmer and more comfortable to sit on.

Make sure that any wooden toilet seat you purchase is well sealed so it can be effectively washed down from time to time with a mild detergent. Also available are jokey and

Left and below **A toothbrush glass can be chosen to complement your bathroom scheme, but it should preferably be unbreakable like this opaque plastic one. Another container frequently found in the bathroom is the laundry basket, essential to hold used towels and items of clothing. The basket should have a lid to cover the contents and be waterproof to withstand the dampness of the bathroom as well as the moisture of the used towels. If your bathroom is small and you feel that a rigid container would take up too much space, a fabric laundry bag with a drawstring top can be hung behind the door.**

decorative toilet-seat covers made in transparent plastic into which seashells, sand, coins, and any number of things have been arranged before the plastic has set. These can be amusing if you are following a flight-of-fancy decorative theme in your bathroom, or as a focus of interest in a small half-bath.

Toilet-paper roll-holders are a functional necessity, but even here there are choices to be made. There is the basic plastic or wooden tube that runs through the center of the roll and telescopes on a spring to allow the roll to be clipped in and out of the frame. Such holders are a bit tricky to use, and the spring can become stretched or broken, which makes the whole mechanism inoperable.

The least complicated and most effective version is the metal cross bar. You simply slip the roll onto the bar, and the slight return at the point keeps the roll in place. If you want to keep a few rolls handy, store them in a small wicker basket or on a plain wooden pole on a base that stands on the floor and can be used to support a vertical stack of rolls.

Above and right **Plastic bins or baskets are available in many colors, and wood is a timeless classic that is suitable for the majority of decorative schemes.**

Top right **This innovative rack for storing toilet paper probably began life as a rack for mail. The rack's wire-mesh construction means that plenty of air can circulate around it, preventing it from rusting, and the rolls from becoming damp, as a result of frequent exposure to steam and moisture.**

Top and above **Simplicity and elegance characterize these two slip-on holders for toilet rolls.**

Right **Traditional and contemporary wall-mounted bar towel rods flank a more decorative towel ring.**

Towels and mats

Towels can be regarded as an accessory in a bathroom. Neatly stacked and folded, they can bring color and texture to a room as well as being inviting to wrap yourself up in.

There are a number of types and textures of towels, ranging from the coarser linen and natural cotton types, which are invigorating after a morning shower and absorbent and light next to the skin, to velvet-pile towels, which are thick and plush, and envelope and absorb water rather than stimulate the skin. The choice of color is almost limitless, but if you like white towels, which feel the cleanest and look wonderful in a generous stack, make sure they stay white rather than absorbing various shades of pink and gray from being mistakenly put in a colored wash.

Terrycloth is often used for bathmats, which are generally chosen to coordinate with bath and hand towels. Cork mats are also good, especially when you step out of the shower, and they feel soft and warm underfoot. Cork mats should be pretreated so they are water-resilient rather than absorbent. Another option is a duckboard, which should be placed on a tiled or linoleum-covered floor because water will run straight off the body, through the open wooden framework and onto the floor.

The Japanese taoru wash cloth is a skimpy towel for mopping the brow; it is also rolled up and used for scrubbing the body, then unfurled, rinsed, and squeezed so it can help to mop off surplus water after bathing. The equivalent in the West would be a face cloth, but our more familiar little towelling squares are not substantial enough to cope with all these demands.

Towel rods

Unheated towel rods are available in wood, plastic, or metal in the form of a ring or a simple bar held in place by two brackets. These towel rods can be attached to a wall beside the sink or on the front or side of a cabinet. The rod allows the towel to dry more efficiently after use because it has space for the towel to be spread out; in a ring the material of the towel is restricted and folds over on itself time and again, which means that it stays damp longer.

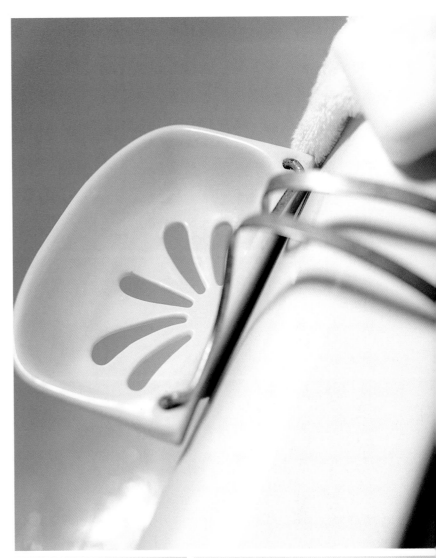

Top right **A soap dish hangs over the side of the bathtub, remaining attached by means of a simple arched metal bracket. Its perforations resemble stylized flower petals. To permit water to drain away easily from wet soap, soap dishes need to have a perforated base. If the dish has no water outlet, the wet soap will melt and form a slimy residue in the base.**

Right **This shelf tray is ideal for a shower enclosure. It has been mounted in the corner of two tiled walls, and any water from the shower or soap will pass straight through.**
Far right **This stylish holder has substantial gaps between the metal supports so is more useful for holding large items such as sponges, loofahs, and face cloths rather than slippery bars of soap.**

4

surfaces and decoration

walls and surrounds

flooring

color

display

THE POPULARITY OF CLASSIC WHITE FIXTURES MEANS THAT THE CHARACTER OF

A BATHROOM IS USUALLY DEFINED BY THE DECORATION, FLOORING, AND FINISHES

TO WALLS AND OTHER SURFACES. THE GROUNDWORK IS EXTREMELY IMPORTANT.

WALLS SHOULD BE CLEANED, PREPARED, FILLED, AND SANDED TO THE HIGHEST

STANDARDS, AND TREATED AND UNDERCOATED SO THE SURFACES ARE SEALED

AND SMOOTH BEFORE PAPER, PAINT, OR TILES ARE APPLIED.

Any chip, crack, or area of peeling paint will become rapidly worse with repeated exposure to the damp

and steamy atmosphere of a bathroom. For safety's sake it is important that surfaces, especially the floor,

should be smooth—uneven tiles may cause you to stub your toe or slip, which could be dangerous.

Furthermore, the surfaces that come into immediate contact with the body are more comfortable if they

are smooth and soft rather than roughly textured.

Bathrooms are often small rooms; sometimes they have no window or only a small one. In these

situations you need to create the impression of space. This can be done by using pale colors and by

keeping pattern to a minimum—an abundance of pattern can make the space seem small and crowded.

Conversely, in a large bathroom you may decide to use darker colors to make the room seem more

intimate. Adding patterned tile borders will also help to break up large plain areas.

Paint is one of the most durable decorative finishes in a bathroom, and there are many types of paint

specially formulated for the bathroom atmosphere. But painted walls don't have to be plain—although

marbling, dragging, and sponging paint effects are now rather dated, there are plenty of other unusual

and stimulating schemes that can be used to bring an unexpected element to bathroom walls. Murals

can be effective and may vary from extravagant, such as the view of an ancient Greek ruin or temple, to thematic, such as an underwater water lagoon scene complete with coral and fish. A trompe l'oeil view through a fake window brings a touch of outdoors inside. Even a simple graded-color effect may be interesting: you can start with the darkest color at the bottom and build up to the lightest near the ceiling, or vice versa—an effect that can also be achieved with ceramic tiles.

Ceramic tiles have long been a standard part of the decorative armory, but developments in the use of materials are opening up new alternatives. Glass, steel, stone, and wood are all now not only acceptable but also desirable. They can be made part of an exciting and unusual scheme for one of the most intimate and indulgent rooms in the house.

You also need to decide what type of flooring to install and to choose the edging and panels for the bathtub and sink. When investigating the selection of the surfaces on the market, try to keep practicality in mind. A rough, dark gray slate may have initial appeal, but think of the difficulty of removing spots of dried toothpaste from the crevices and stray hairs from between the ridges. Smooth surfaces are in general the simplest to wipe down and keep clean and hygienic.

walls and surrounds

Bathroom surfaces should be water-resistant and smooth to touch. Traditionally, the areas that came into most regular contact with water were tiled, and the rest of the room was either coated with paint or hung with vinyl-treated wallpaper. Paint is still popular, but the paint finishes and the variety and sizes of ceramic tiles are changing to keep up with developments in contemporary design.

Left **Skill is needed to cut hard materials such as ceramic tile, slate, stone, and mirror before attaching wall-mounted appliances.**
Below **Where water is plentiful, damp may seep through crevices, so make sure every seam is well sealed.**

Some bathrooms are decorated with wallpaper, but the textured vinyl finishes of the 1970s and 1980s have been overtaken by more subtle stripes and toile de Jouy patterns. Wallpapers are best used in areas away from the main sources of water and steam. They are also suitable for upper parts of the room, such as the wall space above a band of tiles or around the doorway and window, where more air circulates. A small bathroom, in which the area available for papering is limited, may be the place where more colorful or expensive designs are hung, because the impact or cost is restricted by the small amount that can be used.

In addition to the traditional surface coverings, many new materials can be seen in the bathroom. Glass, plaster, stone, and wood are popular in modern schemes. These organic surfaces work well with traditional white fixtures and with hard steel finishes—the tactile and earthy finishes of the plaster and stone soften the sometimes aggressive lines and look of the steel.

Plaster is not generally suitable for bathrooms unless it is carefully finished with a waterproof seal—otherwise, the plaster will absorb water and eventually start to powder and shale. Any cracks, even in waterproofed plaster, can absorb moisture and become damaged. Walls and surfaces to which plaster is applied should be well prepared, and the finished dry wall should be waxed, varnished, or sealed. Wallboard should be of a type specially designed for use in bathrooms.

Laminated surfaces should be used sparingly and carefully in bathrooms to avoid the "built-in kitchen" look. Some of the strong single-colored finishes are bright and contemporary and can be preformed with smooth curves and soft edges into individual freestanding pieces of furniture.

Where possible, the corners of surrounds, cabinets, closets, and other units should be rounded or capped so hey are not likely to cause injury. When you are planning which materials to put where, remember that cold surfaces such as tiles are best kept at a distance—behind a sink or on the far side of the bathtub—so that, when you are naked, relaxed, and warm from your shower or bath, you won't brush up against or lean on anything that will be cold enough to give you a shock.

Glass

Glass is durable and easy to clean. It can be plain or opaque, colored or clear, but it should be used in a bathroom only if it has been laminated or tempered. Lamination involves sandwiching liquid resin between two sheets of glass. If one sheet of the laminated glass breaks, the other remains intact, and most of the shattered glass remains attached to the sheet by virtue of the laminate to which it is stuck.

Tempered glass is heat-treated to make it four times more durable than standard glass. If and when tempered glass breaks, it crumbles into small lumps rather than sharp shards. In some places, safety glass—which is reinforced by fine lines of wire running through it in a grid pattern—has also been used for bathroom surfaces. This glass has a slight blue/green cast and sometimes comes with a textured finish. Shower enclosures are frequently made of tempered glass; in addition

Left **Tempered glass is not only smooth and easy to clean, but it also has a visual affinity with water. It can be cut and used as a surround for a sink or as a splash protector.** Top and above **Heavy-duty materials such as stone and marble give solidity and opulence to a room and can provide an interesting contrast to plain white ceramic and enameled bathroom fixtures.**

it can be used to create surfaces around sinks and splash protectors around the edges of bathtubs. One advantage of a glass backsplash is that any pattern or design that appears on the wall behind it will show through—so a wallpaper or a handmade collage will be protected but remain visible.

Glass is not in itself an expensive material, but the process of having it cut to size, finished, and erected can be costly. The glass sheets or walls need to be cut to the exact size and the edges polished or rounded off-site, then all the items have to be transported to their destination and assembled. When the glass is in place and secured, the edges and seams, especially in shower enclosures, must be carefully sealed.

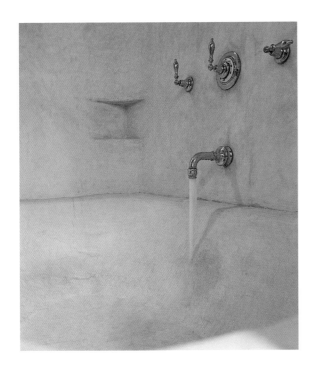

Above **This textural finish has been applied over the walls and outer surfaces of the bathtub, making it look as though it has been hewn from a piece of rock.**

Top right **Stone can be used in many ways. Fine sheets can be applied as façades or panels, and larger blocks or slabs used to form sinks and bathtubs.**

Stone

Stone has good waterproof qualities and comes in many types and finishes. Marble, once found only in rich households, is now more widely and cheaply available in tiles, veneers, and marble and resin composites. The composites are invariably lighter than the pure stone and can have a warmer, slightly softer touch. They are also easier to cut and can be premolded into a number of shapes.

Limestone and granite both come in a choide of muted natural colors, and can be bought in tile form as well as cut to order for a splash protector or sink area. The advantage of specially cut lengths is that there are no seams or gaps that need to be sealed to prevent water from dripping through. The drawback of a stone surface is that any glass or china that is accidentally dropped on it will almost certainly crack or break, and if you knock against it with bare skin, you may suffer bruising.

Wood and fiberboard

Like plaster, wood provides an attractive soft finish in a bathroom, but it should be carefully selected for its water resilience and protectively treated. Constant contact with water can cause kiln-dried and naturally dried wood to split, and water may stain and mark an unfinished or a natural surface. Although there are many paler woods available, the current fashion is for dark wood. Teak is an endangered species, but rubberwood, iorko, and merbau are acceptable substitutes. Many tropical woods have inherent water-repellent and antibacterial properties.

Wood is generally best kept at a distance from detergents, especially those containing bleach. Wood soaps are useful for cleaning; alternatively, a clean damp cloth will remove surface buildup. For woods that lack good water tolerance, it is necessary to seal the surfaces exposed to water with a polyurethane finish, yacht varnish, or one recommended by the lumber yard or carpenter.

Another popular surface for bathroom walls and cabinets is tongue-and-groove wood paneling. This type of finish—which can be painted, or left plain and sealed to achieve one of a variety of looks—creates a homey environment. Tongue and groove can be used to conceal unsightly items, from uneven walls to ugly pipework and toilet tanks. If the bathroom is large, cladding the walls below dado height with tongue-and-groove paneling will have the effect of making it seem smaller and cozier.

Another material suitable for surface building in a bathroom is medium-density fiberboard. It can be routed to create panel-like sections similar to tongue and groove or recessed panels. You can buy or make fancy edging strips—in scalloped shapes, for example—to bring pattern and a decorative finish to a frieze, the top of a cabinet, or the side of a bathtub. Fiberboard must be well sealed and finished.

Metal

Sheets of stainless steel can be lightweight, water-resistant, and molded to form a seamless sink and backsplash in one. Bath panels can also be preformed. But too much stainless steel can make a bathroom appear cold and inhospitable; it should be mixed with natural materials and softened by the use of color, either on the walls or in accessories. Stainless steel should be cleaned with a soft cloth and an abrasive-free cream or aerosol product. Small bits of grit or wire can mark the surface and change a gleaming smooth finish into a maze of tiny scratches that will eventually create a dull, worn appearance.

Paint

Most leading paint manufacturers now make lines of paint suitable for bathrooms, including flat, eggshell or satin, and semigloss. Surfaces covered with acrylic paints are easy to wipe clean with a cloth and a mild detergent. An anticondensation paint is

Above right Shades of white and soft sandstone are combined in a scheme that is clean but warm. Painted surfaces are available in a myriad of colors as well as in a number of vinyl and waterproof finishes. Varying the size of tiles can introduce pattern. For example, you could place large tiles on the floor and smaller, patchworklike ones of the same color on the walls. The variety in size creates a variety of focus. Right The paneling of the cabinets in the foreground and beyond echoes the checkerboard design formed by the tiles on the floor and wall and in the bath panel.

Left The reflective quality of the mirror on the cabinet and splashback contrasts well with the solid, matt appearance of the sink and wall surface.
Bottom left The jigsawlike quality of this wood paneling adds interest and color to the room.

The grain of the wood runs in different directions, and the panels are in a variety of sizes.
Below A crazy paving of flagstones creates a rough interior to this shower. The various shades of the stone and the haphazard shapes add to its appeal.

available that reduces buildup of condensation and contains a fungicide to protect the surface against mold growth. This sort of paint is ideal for use around a shower enclosure with an open top, where steam rises and cools, covering the wall with rivulets of moisture.

As in any other room, the surfaces to be painted must be carefully prepared to achieve a smooth finish, but where there will be a lot of steam and condensation, especially around the sink, shower, and bathtub areas, the preparation should be carried out with extra care. Any cracks, chips, or uneven patches may lead to the paint lifting or chipping—a problem that is aggravated by hot, damp conditions. There are many finishes that can be achieved with paint, but in a bathroom, where wallpaper borders are vulnerable to peeling and damage, painted stencil patterns can be a good alternative. Many companies make stencil kits with precut shapes and a selection of brushes and sponges with which to apply the paint. The stencils can be applied in a band around the top of the ceiling, as a dado rail, or even in a line above the baseboard. But avoid using them in all three places. Be sparing with this type of decoration—otherwise, it becomes intrusive and messy.

Tiles

Ceramic tiles have long been a standard wall covering for bathrooms. Particularly popular today are the small mosaic tiles that come in strips with removable backing for easy positioning and mounting. The mesh or brown paper backing can simply be cut with a pair of scissors or a sharp knife and the unwanted section of tiles put to one side for later use. Attached to the upper surface of the tiles, the mesh also means that the strips of tiles are placed at regular distances apart. Once the reverse side of the tiles have been laid and cemented in place, the mesh is removed.

Mosaic tiles can be used to create many different patterns or pictures. Some images, like those seen on the floors of the sites of ancient Romans baths, are of gods and emperors; others are simple bands of geometric pattern. Another interesting effect can be achieved by starting with a very pale shade at the bottom of the wall and building up to a deep intense shade of the same color at the top. This can be achieved in regular bands of color or in a random, wavelike pattern.

If you are laying standard-sized tiles (4 x 4 inches), try making a pattern with plain tiles rather than using surface-patterned or transfer-decorated tiles. For example, square tiles can be placed on their points to form diamonds. Rectangular, brick-shaped tiles can be set in regular lines or staggered

so they overlap. Mixing shapes and colors can also be interesting. A simple checkerboard effect can be produced with traditional black and white tiles or with light and dark shades of the same color. If placed at the top and bottom of a wall of square tiles, lines of rectangular tiles can be used to give the impression of a dado and baseboard; a similar arrangement of diamond and square tiles in two or three shades of the same color can also create an unusual and attractive effect.

As an alternative to the traditional factory-made glazed ceramic tiles, there are unique hand-made and painted designs. Some of these have objects or pieces of metal pressed into them. Glass tiles are also available in a rainbow of colors.

Matte effects include encaustic tiles, where the pattern is made from inlaying contrasting colors of clay in the surface of the tile. This style of decoration was first used in medieval church and monastery flooring, but has been updated to provide innovative designs with natural, non-gloss, stonelike finishes.

Opposite page, far left **If you have large windows and good access to natural light, dark surfaces can be interesting, but they may be claustrophobic in a small, badly lit room.**

Opposite page, top left **Carrying the mosaic theme through from the floor to the lower half of the wall and the area around the bathtub creates a dividing line between the upper, clear part of the room and the lower area, where the fixtures are plumbed in.**

Opposite page, below left, and this page, left and above **If grouting between tiles discolors with age and wear, it can be cleaned or replaced. An alternative is to tint the grout before you apply it so it reflects the color of the tiles. This will make it less obvious than white and less likely to show stains and marks.**

Ceramic tiles are still one of the most widely used surfaces in bathrooms. They come in a variety of shapes and sizes, and in an almost infinite choice of colors. Although the shiny glazed finish has been dominant for some time, matte finishes are becoming more popular—many have an earthy, organic, stonelike quality that appeals to contemporary designers.

Right These plain rectangular tiles, reminiscent of bricks, have a 1930s feel. They may also recall hospitals and other clinical environments, so they should be used with care and teamed with accessories that soften the utilitarian effect.

Below This multicolored panel and splash protector also uses brick-style tiles, but the strong colors banish any clinical overtones and the shape of the tiles echoes that of the red bricks used in the adjacent wall.

Below right Small tiles are easier than large ones to apply to rounded surfaces.

Opposite page, top A band of tiles, the same size and color as those used on the wall, has been used to create a border beneath the rim of the bathtub.

Opposite page, far right Special edging strips can be used to seal and get around corners where cutting and butting up individual tiles is too difficult.

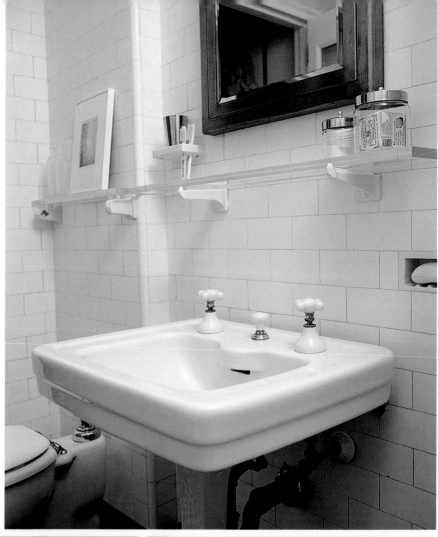

If your bathroom tiles are in good condition but the wrong color, or if you just want to give the place a new look, use a preparation formulated to cope with tile surfaces. Ordinary latex is hard to apply to the shining glass finish and, even when dry, will easily scratch off or peel.

Existing tiles can be painted over and given a new look with specially devised primers and paints. The primer is a base coat that creates a surface to which the paint can adhere. Once dry, the scratch-resistant top coat can then be applied. There are also paints that will cover melamine surfaces, which have a similar shiny finish to tiles. You can update marble-effect or patterned melamine by painting it a plain strong color. Again, a primer must be applied to a clean, dry, dust-free surface. The top coat may be applied when the primer is dry.

The grouting between tiles is an area where grime can gather and discolor the seams. This is particularly noticeable when white or pale-colored tiles have been used. Rather than raking out the existing grout and re-doing it, you could try a specialist device such as a grout pen. This is an applicator containing a paint-based solution that can be easily and simply drawn over the grouting to refresh and brighten it.

When you need to apply grout, choose classic white, which looks clean and fresh. Gray grout can seem dirty next to pale colors, and strongly colored grouts date quickly. White is also less intrusive and means that the tile has more decorative prominence than the utilitarian filler.

Flooring should be durable, waterproof, and nonslip. In many simply furnished and unadorned modern bathrooms, the flooring has also become the focus of color and decoration. Lighter shades help a small space to appear larger, and a dark color makes a large space look warmer and more intimate.

flooring

Bathroom flooring must be able to withstand repeated exposure to water and steam. Seams should be kept to a minimum and away from the center of the room. If possible, lay the flooring before the tub is installed— if you have a rolltop with claw feet, for example, you will be able to see under the tub, where the flow of the floor covering should be uninterrupted.

Many bathrooms are small rooms, so a single color on the floor will give an impression of space; a heavily patterned linoleum or vinyl-tile design will be too busy and overpowering. The main problem with dark flooring in a bathroom is that it shows up dust, talcum powder, and light-colored hairs that are not so visible on paler

coverings. When selecting a floor covering, think of comfort, safety, and hygiene as well as color and pattern. It is worth visiting showrooms and commercial flooring outlets as well as the usual home-construction retailers so you are aware of all the options. Carpet is one possibility, but cork, wood, rubber, linoleum, and vinyl flooring are much better options because they are easy to clean as well as being comfortable under bare feet.

Carpet and matting

Although carpet has sometimes been fashionable as a bathroom floor covering, providing a feeling of luxury and softness underfoot, it is generally best avoided. If you want to put carpet in a bathroom, chose a variety that is rubber-backed and preferably wool or other natural fiber rather than synthetic. Acrylic and nylon stain easily unless protected with a stain-resistant finish. They can also generate a lot of static electricity. If carpet is laid in a large, well-ventilated room, any buildup of moisture and dampness will evaporate quickly. However, if a carpet is to be laid in a small bathroom, you need to install an exhaust fan or some form of ventilation—otherwise, mold may form and the carpet backing will start to rot.

Carpet is difficult to clean thoroughly. Hairs, nail clippings, and sloughed-off skin may become entangled in the pile, and any spilt bath product, oil, or nail polish is

Far left **The square insets in this diamond-patterned tile floor lift the simple layout and add another color.**
Left **This wooden floor has a warm color but is pale and** reflective, giving an overall light appearance.
Above **Wooden floors must be well sealed or finished to avoid splinters and to make them water-resistant.**

quickly absorbed, leaving a stain. Certain areas such as those around the toilet can become marked and odorous. Natural matting materials, such as coir, sisal, and jute, have similar disadvantages to carpet, and some are vulnerable to water damage. The rougher-textured finishes feel prickly underfoot.

Mats and rugs are popular in bathrooms, especially where the flooring is hard and cold. Mats must be carefully positioned and, for safety, should be held in place with rubber backing or carpet grip. The best mats for bathrooms are made from absorbent materials such as terrycloth or cotton. These not only soak up water that drips from the body and feet after showering or bathing, but also can be regularly put into the washing machine and thoroughly cleaned.

Cork

Cork comes from the outer bark of the cork oak, *Quercus suber*, and has the advantage of being a renewable resource because the tree replaces the bark it loses. Cork is a good insulator against cold and noise, and has a soft cushionlike feel underfoot; it is durable and, if sealed, resilient to wear and tear.

The natural color of cork is warm honey-brown. It can be stained or colored in many shades, but it should always be sealed with a polyurethane finish.

Buy cork that has already been impregnated rather than trying to add the sealant once the floor is in place. Flooring that is insufficiently sealed may swell and crack if it absorbs water from a spill or flood.

Cork can be bought as tiles or by the roll. There are various grades of thickness, so make sure you choose the sort that is suitable for floors rather than the thinner product intended for walls. Some tiles are not only impregnated with a water-repellent finish but also have a solid rubber backing, which makes them ideal for the bathroom and increases warmth and sound insulation.

Wood

Bare wood is not an ideal bathroom floor covering because it can be damaged by water and extremes of temperature, but if the wood is treated, seasoned, and sealed, it can provide a natural and versatile surface. The color of a wood floor varies according to the type of tree it comes from. Expensive hardwoods such as elm, ash, walnut, oak, and maple are best left in their natural color so that their intrinsic beauty and the pattern of the grain will show through.

Cheaper softwoods such as pine can be decorated with paint washes and stains—a technique that may also be used to revive damaged or time-worn wooden

Below **The area around the toilet should have an easy-to-clean surface, such as this decking, which can be washed with hot water.**
Right **Wood intended for use in a bathroom, especially on a surface that will often be wet, needs to be specially prepared and finished.**

Right **Wooden decking is warm underfoot and can be laid over a floor made of stone or a similar cold material. In this bathroom there is a stone floor in the shower, which is warmed by cascades of hot water. However, the floor outside, where the bather stands to get dry, is made of wood, making it comfortable to touch with bare feet. The floor area in front of the sink is also made of stone, but someone standing there is more likely to be dry and wearing slippers.**

Below **Rubber matting used to be confined to public thoroughfares and industrial sites, but is now often seen in home bathrooms. It is hard-wearing and water-resistant.**

Right **Stone floors need to be very carefully laid. The cutting, especially in corners, should be accurately done, and the joints should be small, neat, and regular. The gaps between the stone slabs must be sealed to prevent water from seeping under them and rotting the boards or joists beneath.**

floors. To create an all-over whitewashed effect, apply a wash of white paint diluted with mineral spirits or water to a clean floor surface with a wide brush or sponge. Apply one coat at a time and let it dry thoroughly so you can assess the depth of color before applying any additional coats. It is easier to put on two or three coats to build up the strength of a color than to reduce the intensity of a color as it is soaking into the surface of the wood. With a pickled finish, the grain of the wood should be clearly visible; the aim is to convey a hint of color rather than a slab of solid paint.

By using two or three colors of wash, you can create a checkerboard effect on the floor. In addition to diluted paints, stronger and richer shades can be achieved with specific wood stains and dyes. Stencil patterns can also be used to introduce border interest, but let the base color dry thoroughly before applying the next or adjacent color—otherwise, the two colors may bleed and run into each other.

Pickled, stained, and painted floors should all be finished with a water-resistant sealant such as gloss or matte varnish. For a really durable finish, choose marine varnish—used to seal the wooden decks of boats—but you may need to apply several coats to build up a waterproof seal. Marine varnish takes a long time to dry, as does the more usual polyurethane varnish. But doing the job properly will result in a long-lasting and hard-wearing finish. Existing wooden floors can also be sanded and painted, but make sure you seal them again with several coats of varnish or recommended finish.

Wooden floors come in a variety of shapes and styles, from planks to parquet. If you are planning to lay a new wood floor, ask the supplier which type is best for your circumstances, taking into account not only cost but also the size and character of the room. By laying planks parallel to the length of the room, you can make it appear longer;

Right **If you are installing a bathtub on legs, lay the floor first and then put the tub on top to avoid the problem of having to tile around the legs. If the side of the bathtub is destined to be paneled, the flooring can be laid up to the edge of the tub and the panel placed over it for a neat seam.**
Above right **Water sprays in all directions in an open shower room, so the walls and floor are not the only areas that need to be sealed.**
Far right **The corner is where many tiles meet; water may also cascade down the walls at that point, building up a small reservoir.**

if you lay the planks across the width, the room will seem wider. Another interesting way to achieve a pattern with a plain wooden floor is to lay the planks in a line from the corner of the room so they are diagonal to the walls.

Ask the lumber or varnish supplier about the best way to maintain and clean the surface of the floor. Wooden floors are easy to sweep clean and can be mopped with a damp sponge, but some finishes should be cleaned only with a particular recommended product rather than a harsh detergent or bleach, which may cause damage.

Rubber, linoleum, and vinyl

Rubber flooring has traditionally been used for industrial coverings in warehouses, storerooms, and commercial kitchens. Most rubber flooring is textured with a raised pattern or ribbing that creates a nonslip surface.

Available in sheet or tile form, and in a wide choice of colors and finishes, rubber is attached with a strong adhesive to a solid base. If you want to lay it on an existing floor of wooden planks, you may first have to lay a subfloor of wood sheeting or composite so the floor

Left **The mosaic theme seen in the border around the wall has been borrowed to make a small, matlike pattern on the floor.**
Above **Laying diamonds of contrasting color is a subtle but interesting way to break up a plain floor.**
Top right **Dark-colored mosaic wall and floor tiles have been used to give a sense of depth and unity.**
Right **Before laying small tiles, it is crucial that the ground work is done well. If the tiles are laid on floorboards that move, or on an uneven surface, they will lift and crack. Broken tiles both look messy and are potentially dangerous.**
Far right **Black and white checkerboard tiles are a classic floor covering that suits simple schemes in both contemporary and traditional styles.**

Hard flooring

The varieties of hard flooring used in modern designs include concrete, slate, stone, terracotta, and ceramic tiles. Many of these finishes have traditionally been disregarded as bathroom flooring because they are cold underfoot, but the recent vogue for underfloor heating—enjoyed by the ancient Romans—has meant that an ever-increasing number of people are turning to these materials for water-resilient, hardwearing finishes.

Concrete can be laid thinly onto a sealed subfloor and the heating conduits laid in place and smoothed over before the concrete sets. The surface of the concrete can be finished to create a smooth, slightly shiny appearance or lightly textured with a wood-grain effect or simple linear marks. Alternatively, it can be colored with dyeing agents to give a warmer and more homelike appearance or—for something more unusual and exciting—powdered resins can be added to the concrete to give sparkle and luster to what is often regarded as a dull material.

Concrete is durable, waterproof, and easy to clean, but anything fragile that is dropped on it will almost certainly break. The plain appearance of a standard concrete floor can be broken up with mats, rugs, or small sections of wooden duckboard placed in appropriate areas of the floor.

Slate—another natural material that has been shunned as flooring for some time—is now enjoying something of a revival. It, too, has benefited from underfloor heating, and from modern finishes that make it more resilient and less likely to shale or flake. Slate is waterproof and comes in beautiful earthy tones ranging from green and blue-gray to amber pink. The main disadvantage of a slate floor is that it can be noisy when metal or furniture or accessories are dragged or moved over it. Other stone floor coverings such as granite are similarly hard and noisy, but they are also hardwearing and waterproof, and come in a whole spectrum of colors

surface is stable and will not cause the tiles to move and tear over joints. Rubber flooring has a certain amount of sound insulation; it is also water-resistant and can be cleaned thoroughly with a brush or a mop.

Used as a floor covering since the late nineteenth century, linoleum was discontinued for many years until its recent revival. It is made from a combination of natural ingredients—linseed oil, finely ground wood, pine resin, and natural pigments—pressed onto a jute backing. A reasonably flexible product, it is strong, easy to clean, water-resistant, and relatively warm underfoot. If you have a linoleum floor, be careful to prevent water from seeping under the seams or edges because this may cause the jute to absorb water and lift the linoleum off the floor.

Vinyl is a chemically manufactured covering available in many colors and patterns. As is the case with certain linoleum products, vinyl flooring can be laser-cut to order to create a wide range of patterns and pictures. Precut patterns and insets are also available. Vinyl comes in a variety of thicknesses and finishes and some, such as cushioned vinyl, are ideal for the bathroom because they have a soft and spongy feel underfoot.

Tiles of rubber, linoleum, and vinyl can be laid by a competent handyperson, but sheets or rolls of these materials may be unwieldy and difficult to maneuver in a confined space. To avoid making a crucial error when cutting and laying a single area of flooring, it is worth paying a little extra to have the floor laid by a professional.

If you decide to do it yourself, make an accurate paper template of the floor, including all the tricky areas, such as those around the pedestals of the toilet and sink. Lay the material flat outdoors or in a larger room, then use the template to cut out the shape of the area you need to cover.

from white to black, with flecks of gold- and silver-colored metals in their seams that give an appearance of luxury. These surfaces are good in a bathroom with a steam cabinet because they will not be badly affected by high temperatures or a damp atmosphere.

Tiles made of materials such as terracotta and ceramic are durable, waterproof, and less expensive than those made of stone or slate. Terracotta tiles can be manufactured with a textured and handmade appearance. The slight roughness of the surface is not unpleasant underfoot and creates a certain level of nonslip safety. Ceramic tiles used on the floor should be of the sort that have been specially made for the purpose rather than those meant for use on walls or work surfaces, and they may be more satisfactory with a matte rather than a shiny finish. Shiny tiles can become slippery when wet, creating a source of potential danger.

Although usually used in walls or to build semiopaque panels, glass bricks can also be inset into a floor. In an area overlooking a stairwell or an extension cantilevered over a lower floor, glass bricks can be used to give a light and airy appearance. They are especially effective in an otherwise windowless room.

Mosaic is another water-resistant and decorative floor covering. Again, it was the ancient Romans who pioneered the use of mosaic tiles, to adorn the interiors of their bath houses. Mosaics can be made from stone—even from pebbles, although they tend to be

Left **A classic mosaic pattern, modeled on those found in Roman bath houses or villas, uses the colors that have been chosen for the paint work and marble panel of the bath. The floor is the only source of pattern in an otherwise plain scheme.**
Above **A detail of the mosaic floor shows how the tiny sections form a pattern in addition to the pattern created by the colored design.**
Right **In a more modern interpretation of mosaic, the floor and wall have been covered with rectangular sections of tile in a variety of shades of the same color and cut in a variety of widths.**

knobbly to walk on—and glazed matte or vitreous glass tiles. Laying a mosaic picture requires skill and patience. The design must be accurately assembled on the floor, in a dry state, before being set into cement.

If the idea of laying a whole picture strikes you as too daunting, then a small frieze or border, or simply the immediate area under the shower in a wet room, can be decorated to interesting effect.

If you are planning to use any of the heavy hard-floor surfaces, such as stone, marble, or even ceramic tiles, on an upper or

suspended floor, seek the advice of an engineer or an architect before you go ahead. With expert help, you need to calculate the total weight of the flooring plus a tubful of water and figure out if the existing beams are capable of supporting the load without special reinforcement.

color

Color is a very personal thing. Different people respond and react differently to various depths and tones of color, so your choice of decoration must be determined by your own taste or as a joint decision or compromise with your partner or family.

Right **The balance of strong and neutral colors and shades in this bathroom defines each area. The tub and shower feature strong colors, whereas the floor and walls are in pale shades.**

The most effective way to test a color is to apply a good-sized patch of paint, about a square yard, to a wall and live with it for a few days. Walk past it in the morning, look at it in subdued light at night and in full sunlight at midday. If you can get testers in several shades, paint patches in various parts of the room so you can compare them at the same times of day.

Yellow, orange, and red

Some people believe that color can affect your frame of mind and be used to enhance certain moods and periods of relaxation. For example, yellow is a sunny color, and—said to be the first color that the human eye registers—it is also believed to lift the spirits. Yellow tones can vary from the merest hint, which simply warms up white paint, to the powerful impact of a vivid buttercup shade. When choosing a shade of yellow for your bathroom, try it out in different lights. The intensity of color will vary depending on whether it is seen in daylight or in the glow of artificial light. The change can be quite dramatic—from a medium tone of lively yellow to a rich and opulent golden hue.

Orange is a color that inspires either love or hate in most people. It is believed to stimulate the appetite and bring a feeling of warmth—but people with fiery tempers are often advised to avoid living in an environment with too much orange. It is also a fashionable color that may date quickly.

A strong color like orange should be used in moderation in a bathroom. Instead of painting all the walls bright orange, you could paint one or more of the walls in a more muted shade. You could also use a small

Right **The striking, dramatic combination of pink, red, peach, and blue is the sort of color scheme that would transform a dark and windowless room into an exotic, womblike haven.**

Opposite page **This gold and orange crackle-glaze wall has an opulent, luxurious feel. The fragmented effect of the paint finish also complements the marble pillar and the old stone basin. The gold and orange are a warm, rich combination that can** add **to the enjoyment of a relaxing and indulgent soak in the bath.**

Left **The decorative floor and the large framed painting bring together the white and all the earthy tones that have been used elsewhere in the scheme.**

has watery connotations, but some people regard it a cold color, whereas others find it relaxing and tranquil. Some shades of blue have been "hotted" up with a hint of red or yellow making them slightly purple or green. Turquoise, a mixture of blue and green, is a fresh zingy shade, but, like purple, it has a tendency to go in and out of fashion, which may mean that a room painted this color will quickly look dated.

Green is a healing color reminiscent of nature, growth, and rebirth. It can bring a freshness and liveliness to a bathroom in the morning, especially the paler shades such as almond, mint, or apple; but stronger shades such as emerald or malachite look rich and luxurious in subdued lighting—which makes green a color worth considering for a single bathroom that needs to cater for these two moods.

White and cream, brown and black

White, a color associated with purity and spirituality, has long been a favorite in bathrooms—not just for fixtures, but for tiles and paint as well. It provides a neutral background against which colored accessories and decorative items can be placed. It also gives a feeling of freshness and cleanliness. However, too much white can create an atmosphere that is cold and austere, and marks on white paint are instantly noticeable.

Cream and off-white shades combine the clean appearance of white with enough warmth to soften a potentially clinical environment. There has been a trend among paint companies to use primary colors as a base to produce slightly colored whites that are described as, for example, a "hint" of blue or a "hint" of yellow.

Brown is rarely found in bathroom paint or tiles, but in the 1960s and 1970s there was a vogue for chocolate brown and wheat-colored pampas acrylic sanitaryware. Brown is an earthy color with connotations of soil and bark—thought of as dirty and rough, and therefore incompatible with the cleansing activities that occur in a bathroom—but shades of brown appear in wood, which is popular as a decorative surface.

Black may be overpowering if it appears on all four walls, but it can be used to frame a feature or panels, and in borders. Black accessories can also be dramatic against a pale-colored background and when used in tiles combined in a checkerboard effect with contrasting colors such as

amount of a stronger shade in painting the area around a large mirror or window in the form of a frame, making it a secondary element rather than a primary one. Like orange, red—said to signify danger, dominance, and decadence—can be overpowering, especially in a small room. Vivid vermilion can be startling and is best used in moderation, but red mixed with a touch of blue becomes a rich and restful burgundy. Darker shades of red may make a large bathroom feel smaller and more intimate, but it will not create an invigorating place to wash in the morning unless you add plenty of glass, mirror, and chrome to lighten up the overall scheme.

Pink, purple, blue, and green

Pink can be a calming and relaxing color, although the more modern shade of shocking pink is lively and energetic. Shades of pink can give a bathroom a delicate and feminine feel and, because it is at the paler end of the spectrum, pale pink harmonizes well with classic white fixtures.

Purple comes in and out of vogue. Paler shades such as lavender and lilac can, like pink, work well with white fixtures and silver or chrome accessories. Deeper shades of purple make a space feel smaller, and a very dark shade may be oppressive. All sorts of blues are popular in bathrooms—from the palest wash of sky blue to a deep rich navy. Blue

cream or pink. Shiny black surfaces can be difficult to keep clean—soap marks and toothpaste smears have a tendency to show up as white scum or rings, so black tiles and glazed surfaces are not advisable for shower walls or around the sink unless you are prepared to wipe and polish them frequently.

Combining colors

It takes skill to achieve an attractive combination of light and dark colors, and harmony within the tones. Avoid mixing too many colors unless you have deliberately set out to create a rainbow effect.

You can experiment with a small amount of colorful pattern, but make sure that you dilute it with a lot of plain and uniformly colored surfaces. Although colors

Above, above right and opposite page **Mosaic tiles are a good way to introduce a variety of colors into a bathroom. For example, you can bring warmth to a blue room by adding a few purple tiles. To prevent a scheme from becoming too dark,** **sprinkle in a few lighter shades of the main color, or choose a dark color for the lower part of the room and fade in lighter and brighter shades of the same color as the tiles reach the ceiling.** Left **Accessories also can add touches of vivid color.**

from opposing sections of the color spectrum can be brought together to provide an interesting scheme, the choice must be carefully made—because clashing shades may jar and create an unsettling environment.

As a rule, try to choose colors that are within the same family. For example, blue and yellow can be mixed to make green, so those two colors and others closely related to them tend to work well together. Each color comes in many shades and depths of intensity. Using light

Right **Blue is a perennially popular color in bathrooms and shower rooms because of its associations with water. Various shades of blue can used to good effect in both traditional schemes and when combined with modern materials such as the chrome and concrete illustrated here.**

Below **A simple contrasting band of tiles relieves the monotony of a plain wall, and using one of the colors in the checkerboard floor ties the scheme together.**
Right **Shower curtains can be used to introduce color and pattern. The curtain shown here has an outer layer of** dark green velvet, with a paler lining, bringing a sense of luxury to an otherwise simple scheme.
Far right **The standard two-color checkerboard pattern can be made more complex and interesting by adding more colors and laying them randomly.**

and dark tones of the same main color is another way to broaden the scope of your decorative scheme. For example, if the main wall areas in your bathroom are taupe or toffee-beige color, the ceiling could be painted in a paler shade and the woodwork in a richer one. Darker shades can also be used to create false shadows, which can give depth and emphasis to a feature.

Many contemporary bathrooms tend toward neutral and earthy schemes, using pale colors such as gray, beige, and off-white. These soft shades complement white ceramic fixtures, and there is no stark contrast or disharmony with wood, stone, cement, or glass surfaces.

Using color to achieve different effects

If your room is predominately chrome, glass, or steel—hard, shiny surfaces that may have a cool blue or ice green hue—try adding warmer shades, such as gray and blue with undertones of pink, to counteract the potentially cold effect. To cool down hot colors such as red, orange, and bright yellow, combine them with matte surfaces such as slate, stone, or wood and darker, neutralizing colors such as gray or black.

Colors are often linked with themes—for example, a Mediterranean-style bathroom would have a strong blue and white base, whereas a Caribbean flavor would tend toward terracotta and a warm pink or orange wash. A piece of fabric or a mosaic design may also inspire a color combination that can be reflected in flooring, tiles, and paintwork.

If you are unsure about what colors you want, start with a neutral scheme such as white or cream and then add color to it—maybe a wall of pink or a panel of blue—and see how you feel about the color when you have

lived with it for a while. It is easier to build up a color from a pale base than to lighten one that is heavy and dark. Try to achieve a balance of color intensity between the various parts of the room such as the ceiling, the walls, and the floor. If you have surfaces beside the sink, bathtub, or shower enclosure, these should be included in the equation. If you put dark or rich colors on the ceiling and the floor, the two will be optically drawn together, which will make the space seem smaller. If you paint one wall in a deep shade and leave the others lighter, the dark

darker and more solid, so that it appears to be anchored. In a pale scheme avoid dramatically contrasting dark surfaces such as black marble, which will seem heavy beside a white ceramic sink and bathtub in a white room unless other dark elements—a border or accessories—are included. Look for a softer shade of gray or marble flecked with white that will harmonize with the rest of the scheme.

Introducing color can be one of the most enjoyable aspects of decorating or redecorating your bathroom, but any scheme should be carefully thought out and tested. Experiment on a small scale by photocopying a plan or enlarging a photograph of the room and tracing over it, then coloring or painting in the various areas; this will help you to visualize how the finished room would look.

wall will dominate and appear closer to the observer— an effective way of making a long, narrow room seem squarer. If you paint the walls and ceiling the same color and have a floor covering in a similar shade, there will be little distinction between the various elements of the room. To achieve such an integrated scheme, choose flooring the same color as the walls and ceiling but a tone or two deeper; this will make the ground look

display

The style of objects displayed in a bathroom is usually determined by the overall decorative plan. Framed prints or a shelf of books might be appropriate in an indulgent bathroom, for example, while shells and pebbles could be used to enhance a seaside theme.

Objects placed on the surfaces and sills of a bathroom should be carefully displayed to avoid the appearance of clutter and mess. There is a general rule that odd numbers of items look better in a group than even numbers. If you have an even number of ceramic jars or similar objects, split them up, putting one or three of them a little way from the main group.

There are good reasons for keeping displays and arrangements away from windows. For example, items placed in front of the window may impede the passage of light and restrict access to the window, making it difficult to open and close.

Above left and opposite page **If you plan to display a large number of objects, which would be time-consuming to wipe clean on a regular basis, a glass-fronted cabinet like the one included in this bathroom offers an attractive solution.**
Above and right **Bathrooms are personal and usually private spaces where you can indulge in decorative whims that you might not be able to satisfy in the more public rooms in your home. For example, you could display favorite photographs, prints, or paintings, or a collection of old pottery, jars, or containers, which might also be used for storage.**

Shapes, colors, and textures

Displaying objects of various heights and colors can add interest to a room. Place a tall item at the back of a shelf or ledge, preferably slightly off-center. Mid-height objects can be arranged in front of it and the smallest in the foreground.

Several items in different shades of the same color can be displayed so there is a gradual change in depth of tone. For example, you might have towels ranging in color from dark green to apple green. Stacking them in order according to color shade makes them more visually agreeable.

In an understated, single-colored bathroom one colorful object will be the focus of attention, so it should be well displayed. In a white bathroom, a red towel will stand out, so the towel should be neatly folded or draped rather than crumpled up and left hanging off the side of the bathtub. In a yellow bathroom a single blue glass bottle could be put on a shelf or surface at around eye level so the eye is comfortably drawn to it.

Contrasting textures—mixing rough with smooth and heavy with light—will also add to a display. For example, on a shelving system or shelf room divider, you could place five white towels on one shelf, an opaque glass vase on another, and a bowl of sponges on a third. The velvety warm texture of the towels will contrast with the smooth cool exterior of the glass, which in turn will highlight the uneven, knobbly surface of the sponges.

Do not be afraid of empty space. Sometimes a vacant area can be restful; it may also draw the eye to a different part of the room or to a particular display, and in some cases to a view or decoration beyond. "Less is more," as the saying goes, and this is especially true in a bathroom.

Plants

Plants can help to absorb extra humidity in a bathroom and make the room feel fresh and alive. They introduce a softer element to a room that tends to be full of hard and angular surfaces. Certain varieties with scented flowers not only look attractive, but also add their perfume to the warm air.

Choose plants that enjoy a warm humid environment and, if appropriate, restricted access to daylight. Hardy herbs such as sage, rosemary, and thyme can thrive in the bathroom atmosphere; they are scented and attractive. and can be used in making face packs and hair rinses.

These herbs can be grown in pots and require minimal maintenance. If they begin to look jaded, take them outdoors to recover in daylight for a couple of weeks during the summer.

Orchids that enjoy humidity can add a luxurious and delicate element. Glossy leaved species such as the castor-oil plant will be content in a cooler bathroom, and the sweetheart plant with its decorative heart-shaped leaves is another bathroom-friendly species. Plants that grow well in the absence of direct sunlight include the prayer plant and ferns such as the sword, lace, and feather varieties.

Put the plant in a simple, understated container so the plant rather than its pot is the main feature of the display. The color of the container could be chosen to coordinate with the wall or tile color, which will help maintain its anonymity.

Dried flowers and plants are an attractive alternative to living species—and they do not need to be cared for. There are many interesting dried seed pods, grasses, and thistle heads that bring an outdoor element indoors as

Below and right Available in shades ranging from gold to brown, large sponges are not only pleasant to use but also make colorful accessories when dry. Objects that have a natural affinity with water—either the sea or fresh water—will be tolerant of the damp environment of the bathroom.

Bottom Two sponges and a couple of sunbaked starfish relieve the monotony of a narrow shelf.

Left **A classical stone urn with an arrangement of hydrangeas softens the expanse around a plain sink and adds a decorative and indulgent element to what might otherwise be a somewhat clincal effect. Plants and fresh flowers do not generally** respond well to the environment, of a bathroom, but dried flowers, such as these, can survive—although they may need to be dusted from time to time. Take living plants into the fresh air and sunshine to recuperate if they start to wilt in the damp air.

Glass, china, and shells

Where possible, avoid displaying glass or other types of breakable object unless they are safely placed on a high shelf or well out of the way of the accidental flick of a towel or the sleeve or belt of a bathrobe. Glass and china shards can easily cut exposed skin, and it is often difficult to sweep up the tiny splinters that remain on the floor surface or in the pile of a terrycloth mat after a breakage.

Placing breakable objects on nonslip or ribbed rubber mats can help to give them extra stability. Alternatively, place them toward the back of a deep shelf. Glass-front cabinets will also keep them carefully out of harm's way, but make sure such a cabinet is in keeping with the general feel of the bathroom rather than resembling a display cabinet that has got lost on its way to the living room or kitchen. Some people hang decorative pieces of china on the walls of the bathroom. These are often chosen

Left **A simple shelf with hooks underneath it offers a practical means of storing and displaying bath-related items. It is ideal for a shower room or steam room, where you may want to brush or pumice the skin during bathing.**
Right **Dried twigs, three plain vases, and a glass decanter make a simple but appealing arrangement on the top of a cabinet.**

well as a touch of color and texture. When purchasing a decorative arrangement, ask if the flowers are treated or varnished. Those that are can withstand the atmosphere of the bathroom; others may fade and droop after repeated exposure to moisture.

When buying colored dried flowers, be careful to check that the dyes are fast because condensation may cause the colors to leach out and drip onto surfaces and fabrics in the room. Also, if you brush up against the flower arrangement when undressed, you may inadvertently (but temporarily) dye your skin.

Far left **A dark background highlights pale-colored items, or those made of glass or chrome, when they are grouped in front of it.**
Left **Shelves of reinforced or laminated glass make a clean, unobtrusive support for any display. Glass objects arranged on glass shelves can be lit from above or below so they glow dramatically in subdued evening light.**
Below **These old pottery vases serve a functional purpose as well as being attractive. Containers of a matching color or design are preferable to a random assortment.**

to reflect the color or theme of the bathroom. For example, if pale blue and white Delft-style tiles have been used for the area around the shower and bath tub, plates, or a number of original antique tiles echoing the color and pictorial finish, may be hung and displayed or stacked on shelves. Similarly, plates with the Willow Pattern can be used in a white and dark blue bathroom. Wall-hung china is often safer than free- standing items because it is hooked or wired to an anchored hook or support. These sorts of displays can be quickly and effectively washed and replaced.

Some people like to exaggerate the watery theme of a bathroom with displays of shells. These can gather dust and, being fragile, are often easily broken.

To display shells attractively but safely, you could consider framing them. Depending of the depth of your biggest shell, you may need a box frame that has added capacity. The shells can then be arranged and stuck onto a painted or colored background, or even a background of sand, and then carefully clipped into the back of the frame.

Sensual pleasures

There are many opportunities in a bathroom to combine visual and aural pleasures. Sensual perfumes such as patchouli, rose, and ylang-ylang can be shown on display but also used. Some essences and perfumes may be stored in attractive clear glass bottles and used directly in bath water or in a massage oil, but others that are sensitive to light will have to be kept in a dark place or in colored glass bottles.

Other ways of using scent to aid relaxation, relieve stress, and help insomnia include burning a joss stick or cones of jasmine or sandalwood. These are best used in a stand or dish that is heat-resistant and will catch the cinders and ash as the stick or cone burns. Scented candles have a similar effect and can be bought in containers that have been specially treated to make them resistant to heat.

Candlelight is a very restful and subtle form of illumination in a bathroom, and the candles themselves can be arranged to form an attractive display. Small votive lights placed in the base of colored glass containers will cause the glass to emit a colorful glow. Votive candles are also relatively safe because the flame and hot wax are kept safely within the tin container.

Wall sconces are another way of bringing candlelight into the bathroom. These can be displayed on either side of the bathtub or in rows one above the other. Wall sconces with mirrored backs double the effectiveness of the candle flame.

In a dressing room or connecting bathroom, you could make a colorful display of silk ties or silk scarves. Hanging silk in a warm moist environment can help to keep it crease-free, as the humidity and temperature will cause the lines and folds to drop out. But remember that, after someone has indulged in a steamy bath, the room should be ventilated to prevent the silk from becoming damp and musty.

One great advantage of displaying small items and objects is that they are not fixed for life. You can always rearrange or vary them to transform a room or give it a fresh look. You may also find that you like to change displays from season to season so that you are in touch with what is going on outdoors. This can be done not simply with practical trappings such as towels and shower curtains, but also with plants and baskets of pine cones or seashells.

Far right **The display of a single stem of a fresh flower in an ornate container with simple pots and bowls on a bamboo tray is an idea inspired by the Orient.**
Right **A decorative bowl is displayed on a cabinet with scroll detailing: the bowl is a sink and the cabinet conceals pipes and unsightly bits of plumbing.**
Below **Guest soaps can be laid out in a small basket lined with a hand towel.**